ACCLAIM FO

"One of the most lively, l ... the American scene, Weigel spe ... confines of Catholic theolo..."

DANIEL JOHNSON, *Commentary*

"The best book to come out on the scandals . . . [Weigel] not only offers a sophisticated treatment of the issues but also has some incisive suggestions for where the Church needs to go from here."

KATHRYN JEAN LOPEZ, *American Outlook*

"All genuine reform must be grounded in re-conversion to Christ, and Weigel's call to deeper holiness is passionate, and has nothing of the saccharine or the sentimental. He offers a heroic vision of the Christian life that is much needed in a time of despair and mediocrity."

CHRISTOPHER J RUDDY, *The Christian Century*

"A valuable book . . . because it represents a new voice in the Catholic Church, the emergence of a new breed of young intellectual conservatives, determinedly Catholic in the traditional sense, absolutely loyal to the vision of Church and priesthood articulated during the pontificate of John Paul."

BRENDAN HOBAN, *The Furrow*

"Riveting. Disagree with him if you will. I question some points myself. But boring the man is not."

JOHN JAY HUGHES, *The National Catholic Reporter*

"The principal strength of Weigel's analysis is that he always looks at the Church through a theological lens which, though it may surprise many lay Catholics, is not always what bishops have done."

FATHER RAYMOND J. DE SOUZA, *National Post*

"Weigel, whose biography of John Paul II is justly admired, has absorbed the teaching and example of the present Holy Father both as to what the Church is and what the place and life of the clergy within it ought to be. In fact, this is, in the end, a surprisingly positive book."

JAMES V. SCHALL, S.J., *Claremont Review of Books*

THE
COURAGE
TO BE
CATHOLIC

*Crisis, Reform, and
the Future of the Church*

GEORGE WEIGEL

BASIC
BOOKS

A MEMBER OF THE PERSEUS BOOKS GROUP
NEW YORK

Designed by Brian Mulligan

*Cataloging-in-Publication Data is available at the Library of
Congress.*

ISBN-10: 0–465–09260–8 (hc)
ISBN-13: 978–0–465–09260–4 (hc)
ISBN 0–465–09261–6 (pbk)
ISBN-13: 978–0–465–09261–1 (pbk)

DHSB   10 9 8 7

For all those who will contribute to the genuinely Catholic reform of the Church in the United States.

You know who you are.

Be not afraid.

CONTENTS

CONTENTS

INTRODUCTION

IN THE FIRST MONTHS OF 2002, the Catholic Church in the United States entered the greatest crisis in its history. When Lent began on February 13, the penitential ashes imposed that day on millions of Catholics felt leaden. Something had gone desperately wrong. Something was broken. Something had to be fixed.

Like every Christian community, the Catholic Church is a Church of sinners. Its spiritual rhythms regularly repeat the ancient biblical cycle of failure, repentance, penance, forgiveness, and reconciliation. Yet even in a Church that knows a lot about sin, some acts of wickedness still retain their capacity to shock. The sexual abuse of minors by priests—men traditionally called "Father"—is one such kind of wickedness. So is the failure of bishops—shepherds, in the ancient image— to guard the flock against predators, especially predators from within the household of faith. The shock of seemingly wide-spread clerical sexual misconduct, reported on an almost daily basis in the first months of 2002, was immeasurably intensified by what even sympathetic Catholics had to regard as some bishops' inept and irresponsible response to grave sins and crimes. In this instance, one plus one yielded something more than two: one plus one equaled an unprecedented crisis.

In the language and thought-world of the Bible, "crisis" has two meanings. The first is the familiar sense of the word: the venerable *Webster's Seventh Collegiate Dictionary* defines a "crisis" as "the turning point for better or worse in an acute disease or fever . . . a paroxysmal attack of pain, distress, or disordered functions . . . an emotionally significant event or radical change of status in a person's life." Throughout the first half of 2002, the Catholic Church in the United States certainly seemed to be in "crisis," according to those definitions. The second meaning of "crisis" in the Biblical world is instructive, however: a "crisis" is also a great time of opportunity, an invitation to deeper faith, a summons to a more thorough conversion.

The premise of this small book is that we best understand the current crisis in Catholic life in this second sense—as a tremendous opportunity. An opportunity for what? An opportunity to deepen the reforms the Catholic Church begun by the Second Vatican Council in 1962–1965, which are precisely the reforms urged by Pope John Paul II throughout his entire pontificate.

Like virtually everything else in Catholic life, the very word "reform" has been bitterly contested since Vatican II. Those usually identified as Catholic "reformers" would, in at least some instances, be more accurately described as a wrecking crew for whom nothing short of Catholicism's transformation into a kind of high-church, politically correct American "denomination"—Catholic Lite—will suffice. At the other end of the spectrum, Catholics of a more traditional bent have shied away from the word "reform" and its powerful connotations of the Protestant Reformation, preferring a word like "renewal" to describe what they think Vatican II intended and John Paul II intends. In light of the two-edged scandal of clerical sexual abuse and episcopal malfeasance, perhaps everyone in the Catholic Church—including that broad group of faithful Catholics for whom the ecclesiastical tong-wars are of far less interest than the sacraments and the local parish—can now agree that what the Church needs is *reform*.

What, then, is genuinely *Catholic* reform?

A Church with almost two thousand years of history behind it has inevitably passed through many moments of crisis and many moments of reform. In each instance when crisis-as-cataclysm has been transformed into crisis-as-opportunity, "reform" has meant a return to the Church's roots in order to better engage the spirit and the needs of a given time and place. "Reform," in the history of the Catholic Church, has meant retrieving, renewing, and developing often-forgotten elements of the Church's tradition. It has not meant rejecting the past, or severing the present and the future from the past. Genuine "reform" in the Catholic Church has always meant returning to the past—to roots—in such a way as to create the possibility of a genuinely new future.

That is what happened in what we now know as the Dark Ages, when the collapse of the Roman Empire threatened the very survival of the Christian West: The reform led by great monks and nuns such as Saint Benedict and Saint Scholastica created new forms of Christian discipleship and, in doing so, saved the Church's memory—and Western civilization. That is what happened in the early Middle Ages, when a decadent clergy threatened the Church's mission: The reforms launched by Pope Gregory VII revived early penitential practices and reached back to such ancient traditions as priestly celibacy in order to prepare the Church for a nobler future. That is what happened in the sixteenth century, when the Protestant Reformation fractured western Christianity: The Council of Trent (1545–1563) unblushingly examined the Church's corruptions and failures, restated the fullness of Catholic truth, and made that tradition the basis of a thoroughgoing reform of seminaries, the priesthood, the episcopate, the Church's worship, and indeed almost every facet of Catholic life.

And that is precisely what Vatican II proposed: to "update" Catholicism for the twenty-first century by retrieving the deepest taproots of Catholic faith in the Bible, the great Church Fathers of the first millennium, and the medieval theological masters. By returning to these sources of Catholic faith, the bishops of Vatican II hoped, the Catholic Church would be able to preach more effectively the passionate love of God for all humanity, made visible in the incarnate Son of God, Jesus Christ, crucified and risen. By rediscovering its roots, the Catholic Church would better offer Jesus Christ to the world—Jesus Christ, the answer to the question that is every human life, as John Paul II has described the Church's Master.

Every great period of reform in Catholic history has involved a thorough reform of the priesthood and the episcopate. That is one of the things that is self-evidently required today if the promise of Vatican II is to be fulfilled. To grasp what is at stake, as well as the meaning of genuine reform, Catholics need only look back about five hundred years. In 1512–1517, the Fifth Lateran Council met in Rome. It was intended to be a great reforming Council. It failed. Why? Because its analysis of the Catholic crisis at that moment was shallow; because the reforms it proposed were either inadequate in themselves or inadequately implemented; and because the Church's bishops, including the reigning pope, lacked the will and the courage necessary to do the needed job. The failure of Lateran V was the prelude to the Reformation, which shattered the unity of the Christian West and set in motion the dynamics that eventually led to the European wars of religion. Failures of reform carry a high cost.

No one knows whether, in the twenty-fifth century, Vatican

II will be remembered as another Lateran V—a reforming Council that failed—or another Trent—a reforming Council that was so successful that it set the course of Catholic life for more than four hundred years. The pontificate of John Paul II has been a heroic effort to ensure that Vatican II—which made a profoundly Christian analysis of the crisis of human civilization at the turn of a new century and a new millennium—becomes a second Trent, not a second Lateran V. The question is not whether Vatican II adequately analyzed the Church's situation. The question is whether that analysis has been correctly understood and vigorously implemented. The current crisis in the Catholic Church in the United States has made unmistakably clear just how much work even so dynamic and effective a pope as John Paul II has left the rest of the Church to do.

Individual Christians fail when we avert our gaze from Christ and start looking elsewhere for security. Like Peter in the gospels, we, too, can "walk on water"—but only so long as we keep our eyes fixed on the Christ who beckons us to do what we imagine to be beyond our capacities. The same applies to the Church. At the bottom of the bottom line, every crisis in the Church is a crisis of fidelity. And the answer to a crisis of fidelity is fidelity: a deeper conversion to Christ, a more thoroughly Catholic reform of Catholicism. Amid the many complexities of the Catholic crisis of 2002, which will be explored in what follows, a great simplicity stands out: This is a crisis of *fidelity*.

Crisis means trauma; crisis also means opportunity. The

trauma of the Catholic Church in the United States in 2002 will become an opportunity to deepen and extend the reforms of Vatican II if the Church becomes more Catholic, not less—if the Church rediscovers the courage to be Catholic. The answer to the present crisis will not be found in deconstructing Catholic faith or further loosening Catholic discipline. The answer to the present crisis will most certainly not involve the Catholic Church surrendering to the decadence of the sexual revolution, as so many other Christian communities have. Such surrenders, and the tremendous human suffering they cause, are one of the sources of the crisis, not a solution to it. The answer to the current crisis will not be found in Catholic Lite. It will only be found in a classic Catholicism— a Catholicism with the courage to be countercultural, a Catholicism that has reclaimed the wisdom of the past in order to face the corruptions of the present and create a renewed future, a Catholicism that risks the high adventure of fidelity.

The Catholic Church learned the truth about reform from its parent, Judaism, for the pattern of authentic Catholic reform first took shape in the Hebrew Bible. There, the prophets insisted that the answer to Israel's whoring after other gods was neither greater subtlety in the worship of false gods (Idolatry Lite), nor more clever ways to cover one's theological bets (Syncretism Lite), but rather radical fidelity to the one true God and His commandments. Similarly, crises of fidelity in the Catholic Church are never remedied by Catholic

Lite, but only by more radical fidelity to the fullness of Catholic faith. That is the truth the current crisis is compelling the Catholic Church to remember—and to act upon.

What today's Catholic crisis is, how it came about, and how the crisis might become a great moment of reform is the business of this book.

CHAPTER ONE

WHAT THE
CRISIS IS

THE FIRST CATHOLIC SETTLERS in the original thirteen colonies landed on St. Clement's Island in the Potomac River, south of present-day Washington, D.C., on March 25, 1634. In the ensuing 368 years, the Catholic Church in the United States never experienced anything like the first six months of 2002:

~ On January 6, 2002, the *Boston Globe* reported that a former priest, John Geoghan, had been credibly accused of sexually abusing more than 130 young boys over a period of some thirty years. During that period, Boston archdiocesan officials assigned Geoghan to three different parishes, assured in each instance by therapists that Geoghan had been "cured."

With lawsuits still pending, settlements to Geoghan's victims had already cost some $10 million. In February, Geoghan was sentenced to nine to ten years in prison after conviction on a charge of indecent assault against a ten-year-old boy.

～ On January 29, the Diocese of Tucson settled eleven civil lawsuits alleging sexual abuse of sixteen plaintiffs by four priests (two of whom were still living). One incident of abuse took place in 1989, with the rest taking place in the period 1967–1976. Damages were estimated in the millions of dollars.

～ On January 31, the *Boston Globe* reported that molestation claims had been settled against "at least 70 priests" who had served in the Archdiocese of Boston over the past fifty years.

～ On February 2, the Archdiocese of Boston removed two priests from their parish assignments eight days after the Archbishop of Boston, Cardinal Bernard F. Law, had "asserted that all priests known to have been accused of sexually molesting minors" had been dismissed from work in parishes.

～ On February 15, the Diocese of Manchester, New Hampshire, announced that local prosecutors had been given the names of fourteen priests accused of sexual abuse; seven had already been suspended from their ministry, and the others were suspended that day.

～ On March 3, Father Michael Pecharich, an Orange County, California, priest, said goodbye to his parish after admitting that he had molested a teenage boy in the early 1980s.

～ On March 4, the *Los Angeles Times* reported that Cardinal Roger Mahony had directed "as many as a dozen Southern

California priests who were involved in past sexual abuse cases . . . to retire or otherwise leave their ministries." Mahony's refusal to release the numbers of names of priests involved and the history of their assignments led to widespread criticism. Inter-office e-mails between Mahony and his subordinates, detailing efforts to manage the public relations aspects of the forced resignations, were leaked to the local media, read aloud on local radio stations, and subsequently published.

~ On March 6, the *Boston Globe* reported that a Jesuit priest was suspended from teaching at Boston College High School after accusations that he had sexually molested a student twenty years before. The announcement came one day after the disclosure that two other Jesuits had sexually assaulted students at the school in the same period. A day later, according to the *Globe*, "the New England Jesuit Province turned over to Suffolk County prosecutors . . . the names of five Jesuit priests who have been accused of sexual misconduct."

~ On March 8, Bishop Anthony O'Connell of Palm Beach, Florida, resigned his office, admitting that he had sexually abused a fifteen-year-old seminarian in 1975. O'Connell had been assigned to the Palm Beach diocese in 1998 to replace Bishop J. Keith Symons, who had resigned after admitting that he been guilty of the sexual abuse of minors. At the press conference announcing his resignation, Bishop O'Connell acknowledged the possibility that another abuse charge could be made against him, suggested that he had been too influenced by sex-therapists Masters and Johnson during his days at the high school seminary, and asked those who were angry at him to "pray for my forgiveness."

~ On March 17, the *Hartford Courant* reported, on the basis of secret 1999 court documents, that "New York Cardinal Edward M. Egan, while serving as bishop of the Bridgeport Roman Catholic Diocese, allowed several priests facing multiple accusations of sexual abuse to continue working for years—including one who admitted biting a teenager during oral sex."

~ In mid-March, U.S. Attorney General John Ashcroft, reporting on the conclusions of an international child pornography ring, said that those being sought or already arrested included two Catholic priests.

~ On March 23, Bishop Robert Lynch of St. Petersburg, Florida, acknowledged that the diocese had made a $100,000 severance-pay settlement with the bishop's former communications director, who had accused the bishop of sexual harassment; Lynch denied the charges.

~ On March 24, the *Los Angeles Times* reported that two Jesuits, a priest and a brother, had molested two mentally disabled men who worked at a Jesuit retreat center in Los Gatos, California, over a period of decades.

~ On March 26, the Diocese of Cleveland announced that nine priests were under investigation for sexual abuse of minors, while another twelve were "no longer in active ministry" because of similar charges. Father Donald F.

Rooney, who had been accused of molesting a girl in 1980, shot himself.

~ On March 28, the *Chicago Tribune* reported that a priest who had done well-regarded work on a committee monitoring alleged cases of clergy sexual abuse had resigned his pastorate in Winnetka after being accused of "inappropriate sexual misconduct" with a teenager in the 1970s. That same day, Bishop William Murphy of Rockville Centre, New York, announced that he had turned over to local officials the names of priests whose personnel files indicated that they had been accused of sexually abusing minors.

~ Pope John Paul II's annual Holy Thursday (March 28) letter to priests acknowledged ". . . the sins of some of our brothers who have betrayed the grace of Ordination in succumbing even to the most grievous forms of the *mysterium iniquitatis* [mystery of evil] at work in the world." Presenting the papal letter at a Vatican press conference on March 21, Cardinal Dario Castrillón Hoyos, Prefect of the Congregation for the Clergy, brushed aside reporters' questions about the situation in the U.S., suggesting that this was in part an American media frenzy—a suggestion markedly absent from the papal letter. (On March 28, the archbishop of Poznań in Poland, Juliusz Paetz, resigned after charges that he had sexually harassed seminarians. Four days later, on April 1, the bishop of Ferns, Ireland, Brendan Comiskey, resigned after a BBC documentary revealed that he had protected a sexually abusive priest for some years. Three weeks later, a Spanish priest stepped down from his pastorate after his one-time homosexual lover began distributing a videotape of the two men.)

~ On April 4, a Baltimore, Maryland, priest, Father Steven Girard, was removed from his duties after being charged with lying to prosecutors about his meeting with a male prostitute.

~ On April 5, a Rhode Island priest, Father Daniel Azzarone, was indicted on charges of sexual assault; he had been suspended from priestly functions after his arrest on the charges the previous November.

~ On April 8, the *Globe* reported that Paul Shanley, a Boston "street priest" and activist who had defended sex between men and boys at a 1978 meeting of what later became the "North American Man-Boy Love Association," and who had been known to have sexually abused young men in the following decades, had been recommended to the Diocese of Bernardino, California, in 1990 with an official letter asserting that the abuser had had no known difficulties during his years in Boston. Documents obtained by the paper indicated that Shanley had received letters of praise from archdiocesan officials, up to and including the time of his retirement in 1996. On April 10, a *Boston Globe* editorial called on Cardinal Law to resign his office, a position taken by the Boston *Herald* on March 13. That same day, three priests, two from the Boston archdiocese and the director of the Jesuit Urban Center (once identified in *Boston* magazine's "Best of Boston" awards as "best place to meet a mate-gay"), defied archdiocesan policy and issued statements objecting to a Church-supported state constitutional amendment banning so-called "gay marriage."

~ On April 8–9, the president and vice president of the U.S. Conference of Catholic Bishops, Wilton Gregory of Belleville, Illinois, and William Skylstad of Spokane, Washington, along with conference general secretary Msgr. William Fay, met with Pope John Paul II and senior officials of the Roman Curia to discuss the situation in the United States.

~ On April 11, criminal charges were filed against a St. Louis priest, Father Bryan Kuchar, accused of sexually abusing a teenage boy in 1995. In the previous four months, according to the Associated Press [AP], "more than a half-dozen priests have been removed" from active service in the Archdiocese of St. Louis.

~ On April 13, the *Washington Post* reported that Milwaukee Archbishop Rembert Weakland, previously praised for creating a model program for handling allegations of clergy sexual abuse, had transferred a priest—who admitted to molesting a thirteen-year-old altar boy—from one parish to another in 1979, and failed to remove him from the ministry until 1992. In 1979, Weakland had promised the teenager's family that he would never allow the priest to be in a position to harm youngsters again.

~ On April 13, Cardinal Bernard F. Law of Boston arrived in Rome for three days of secret meetings with the Pope and

Curial officials about the situation in the Archdiocese of Boston and the cardinal's future.

~ On April 15, the cardinals of the United States and the officers of the bishops' conference were summoned to an April 22–23 meeting with Curial officials and the American cardinals resident in Rome.

~ On April 16, the AP reported that a Pensacola, Florida, priest, who had pled guilty to drug-dealing from his rectory, had traded drugs for sex "with at least one young man."

~ On April 19, the *San Francisco Chronicle* reported that Cardinal Roger Mahony of Los Angeles had reassigned a sexually abusive priest to a parish while Mahony was bishop of Stockton, California. A victim's lawyer and a psychiatrist both charged that Mahony had known of the priest's record of molestation, which Mahony had denied under oath at the priest's 1998 trial.

~ In mid-April, according to the AP, "a priest in a Las Vegas suburb was charged . . . with fondling, photographing, and massaging teenage boys he was counseling at his parish." The diocese had previously suspended Father Mark Roberts from his parish on January 30.

~ On April 22, the *Los Angeles Times* reported that an American cardinal, widely believed to be Cardinal Mahony, would urge Cardinal Law's resignation at a Vatican meeting on April 23–24. At the end of April, according to the *Los Angeles Times,* Cardinal Mahony and the Archdiocese of Los Angeles "were sued for racketeering, negligence, and fraud by sexually abused men who claim that the Church amounted to a criminal enterprise that protected priests who preyed on young people."

~ On April 22–23, an unprecedented meeting took place at the Vatican involving the heads of three Curial congregations, the American cardinals resident in Rome, the cardinals of the United States, and the officers of the U.S. bishops' conference. In an address to the meeting's participants, Pope John Paul II stressed that "there is no place in the priesthood or religious life for those who would harm the young."

~ On April 26, a Manchester, New Hampshire, priest, Father George Robichaud, was arrested and charged with sexual assault in 1985.

~ On April 29, the *Los Angeles Times* reported that Father Carl Sutphin, accused of molesting four boys, had lived in Cardinal Mahony's residence at St. Vibiana's Cathedral and had been recently reassigned by Mahony to serve as associate pastor at the new downtown Cathedral of Our Lady of the Angels.

~ On May 3, the finance council of the Archdiocese of Boston rejected a financial settlement, estimated at between $15 and $30 million, previously arranged with victims of John Geoghan, on the grounds that the settlement would not leave enough money for the archdiocese to settle other sexual abuse claims. Cardinal Bernard Law said he hoped that "as time goes on" Geoghan's victims would "help in the framing of a wider settlement which can include the victims who have only recently come forward."

~ On May 13, a Baltimore priest on involuntary leave, Maurice Blackwell, was shot by a man who accused him of sexual abuse nine years previously. Blackwell had been returned to his parish, under restrictions, on the advice of a counseling center where he had undergone treatment. Cardinal William Keeler placed the priest on "involuntary leave" after other abuse charges surfaced in 1998.

~ On May 16, Father Alfred Bietighofer, a sixty-three-year-old Bridgeport, Connecticut, priest, committed suicide by hanging himself at St. Luke's Institute, a prominent treatment center for troubled clergy in suburban Washington, D.C.

~ On May 21, twelve sexual abuse lawsuits were filed against the Archdiocese of Louisville, Kentucky. One of those named was a former Louisville priest, J. Kendrick Williams, who had become the bishop of Lexington, Kentucky. Bishop Williams denied the charges but stepped down from exercising his office; his resignation was accepted by the Pope in early June.

~ On May 23, it was revealed (in a breach of a confidentiality agreement) that Archbishop Rembert Weakland of Milwaukee had paid $450,000 in 1998 to a man with whom he seemed to have had a homosexual affair twenty years before. Weakland, who had reached the mandatory retirement age of 75 in early April and was waiting for the Pope to accept his resignation and appoint his successor, said in a statement that he had asked the Vatican to accelerate the acceptance of his resignation. The resignation was accepted the next day.

There is more. But perhaps the point has been made: This is a crisis. Understanding the crisis is the beginning of resolving it.

A THREE-HEADED MONSTER

Amid the steady drumbeat of press reports in the first months of 2002 about sexual abuse by Catholic priests, careful readers could discern three types of such abuse.

Pedophilia—a disordered sexual attraction to prepubescent children—was the most revolting of the three. Because this long-simmering crisis of sexual misconduct and failed episcopal leadership first came to national attention in January 2002 through the case of John Geoghan, a classic pedophile, the press, some bishops, and some Catholic commentators took to describing the crisis in shorthand as a "pedophilia crisis" or a "crisis of child sexual abuse." That was not accurate.

The second form of sexual abuse involved priests having illicit sexual relations with women: some of them minors, others not. It was striking, however, that this age-old problem was not prominent among the press accounts of clergy sexual abuse in the first half of 2002.

According to press reports, confirmed by the studies of reputable scholars, the most prominent form of clergy sexual abuse in recent decades has involved homosexual priests abusing teenage boys and young men. It took many editors, television personalities, and radio talk-show hosts approximately two and a half months to recognize what print reporters had, in fact, been uncovering for months: namely, that the overwhelming majority of cases of abuse did not involve prepubescent children, but rather teenage boys and young men, often in school or seminary settings. While clinical distinctions ("fixated ephebophilia," "regressed" or "stunted" homosexuality) may be useful for purposes of professional study and therapy, normal English describes such abuse as homosexual molestation.

The monster of clergy sexual abuse had three heads. Homosexually oriented priests, seemingly incapable of living the celibacy they had promised to God and the Church, and abusing teenagers and young men committed to their care, form the largest of the three heads.

It is important to recognize that the sexual abuse of minors is not a problem limited to the Catholic Church. On the basis of a survey of adults in the United States and Canada, one prominent psychologist estimates that some 19 percent of today's adult population was subjected to sexual molestation before they were eighteen years old. Researchers and counselors are convinced that most sexual abuse of children and minors takes place within families, and is thus rarely reported. Virtually every major institution in American life has had to face issues of sexual harassment and sexual abuse. Shortly after Easter, 2002, the evangelical Protestant newsmagazine, *World*, reported the cases of three Protestant ministers who had tried to excuse their sexual abuse of women they were counseling (a potential crime in twenty states) on the grounds that the sex involved was "consensual." In May 2002, the Rev. John Lundin, a Lutheran pastor who chairs the Interfaith Sexual Trauma Institute, worried aloud to a reporter about a significant Internet pornography problem among Protestant clergy. Associations of physicians, attorneys, counselors, teachers, and others in the "helping professions" have all adopted codes of sexual conduct—a sure sign that there were problems to be addressed.

And yet the combination of clergy sexual abuse and failed leadership by bishops clearly and unmistakably demonstrates that the Catholic Church in the United States is in crisis.

It is a crisis because *any* sexual misconduct by persons placed in positions of trust and responsibility for the young is wicked and scandalous.

It is a crisis because sexual abuse by priests harms the whole Church. It has scarred young souls and condemned once-trusting young men to miserable lives. It has ravaged families, who have felt not only the initial wound of abuse but the further wound of seeming indifference from some bishops. A priest guilty of sexual abuse is a man who has broken vows he pledged before the entire Catholic community, and in doing so he has hurt the entire community—just as any sexual misconduct wounds the entire community.

It is a crisis because clergy sexual abuse had done serious damage to the Church's reputation and its ability to be a credible moral teacher in a society facing issues (many involving the biotech revolution) with profound ethical consequences. The Catholic Church's ability to help steer the United States away from *Brave New World* is impeded when even a small minority of its priests and some of its bishops behave like the jackbooted abusers and authoritarians of *1984*.

It is a crisis because clergy sexual abuse in any Christian community casts a long, dark shadow over every Christian community's efforts to preach the Gospel of Jesus Christ at the beginning of a new millennium.

It is a crisis because Catholic priests and bishops should know better; and the people of the Church have every reason to expect that their pastors will know better.

The crisis has psychological, legal, even political implications.

At its root, however, it is a crisis of fidelity—a crisis of faith.

A CRISIS OF PRIESTLY IDENTITY

While the Second Vatican Council addressed virtually every issue of contemporary Catholic life in its sixteen documents, including one on the ministry of priests and another on the formation of priests in seminaries, most observers, including many priests, thought that the Council had given rather short shrift to the renewal of the priesthood. The First Vatican Council (1869–1870), which defined the exercise and limits of papal infallibility, had been a council about popes. The Second Vatican Council, which defined the world's bishops as a "college" with and under the headship of the Bishop of Rome, had been a council about bishops, in many respects. What, many asked, about priests?

According to ancient Catholic doctrine, reaffirmed by Vatican II, bishops are the successors of the apostles and enjoy the fullness of the sacrament of Holy Orders. At the same time, Vatican II taught another venerable truth: that ordained priests are "living instruments of Christ the eternal priest." At his ordination, every priest "assumes the person of Christ." The Catholic priest, in other words, is not simply a religious functionary, a man licensed to do certain kinds of ecclesiastical business. A Catholic priest is an icon, a living re-presentation, of the eternal priesthood of Jesus Christ. He makes Christ present in the Church in a singular way, by acting *in persona Christi*, "in the person of Christ," at the altar and in administering the sacraments.

The Catholic priesthood, in other words, is not just another form of "ministry." Ordination to the priesthood in the Catholic Church radically transforms who a man *is*, not just what he *does*. In fact, in the classic Catholic view, the things a priest *does*—the things a baptized lay Catholic cannot do, such as celebrate Mass or forgive sins sacramentally in confession—are entirely dependent on who he *is* by the grace of his ordination. The old *Baltimore Catechism* tried to describe the difference ordination makes by saying that the sacrament of Holy Orders imprinted an "indelible mark" on a man's soul: Once ordained, a man is a priest forever, because he has been configured to Christ the eternal priest in an irreversible way. A still older philosophy would say that a priest is "ontologically changed"—changed in his deepest personal identity—by his ordination. However the difference is described, the key to understanding the Catholic priesthood *as the Catholic Church understands it* is to understand that the priesthood is a matter of who a man *is*, not simply a question of what he *does*.

Too many Catholics in the United States, including too many priests and bishops, seem to have forgotten these basic truths about the priesthood over the past thirty-five years.

In addition to renewing the episcopate and the priesthood, Vatican II eagerly sought to revitalize the distinctive vocation of lay people in the world. Pre-Vatican II Catholic jargon reserved the word "vocation" for priests and consecrated religious men and women—only priests and nuns "had vocations." Not so, taught Vatican II, reaching back to an older tradition. Every baptized Christian has a "vocation," a unique place in God's saving and sanctifying work in the world. The distinctive lay vocation, the Council continued, is to permeate the family and the worlds of business, culture, and politics with the truths of Christian faith.

What the Council did not anticipate was that the priesthood would become somewhat "laicized" and the laity clericalized as the first generation of post-Vatican II Catholics tried to implement the Council's teachings, according to a rather loosely defined "spirit of Vatican II." Clerical lifestyles, seminary discipline, and the interaction of priests and lay Catholics all changed dramatically in the years immediately following the Council. While some of the changes were overdue and welcome, one widespread effect of the changes was to blur the distinctive identity of the Catholic priest. At times, and in more than a few instances, it seemed that the only thing distinctive about the priest was his role at Mass; in dress, lifestyle, and habits of association and recreation, it became difficult to "see" the uniqueness of the priestly vocation in the Church.

Moreover, by the mid–1970s, virtually everything in the Catholic Church was being described as a form of "ministry," to the point where ushers in churches were habitually described as "ministers of hospitality." Ideas have consequences, and so do words. If everything is a "ministry" and everyone in the Church is a "minister" of one sort or another, what, if anything, is distinctive about the ordained ministry of the priest? Doesn't it demean the "ministry" of baptized lay Catholics if the Church continues to insist on the unique "ministry" of the ordained priest?

These confusions had many ramifications. Not least among them was the claim (often heard during the controversy over clergy sexual abuse) that if the Catholic Church insisted that it must be governed by a "hierarchy" composed of ordained bishops and priests (all of whom were men), it was branding itself an authoritarian, misogynist hangover from the Middle Ages. Many Catholics in the United States wondered why, if the Church was what sociologists aptly described as a "voluntary organization," it shouldn't govern itself like most other voluntary organizations—by majority rule, with "offices" open to all members?

In the three decades after Vatican II, and as they experimented with various new forms of liturgy, education, social activism, and Church governance, more than a few Catholics in America lost sight of the fact (clearly taught by the Council) that the Catholic Church is not a *denomination*—an institution whose form is typically defined by the will of its members—but a *Church*—a community whose basic structure and boundaries are defined, once and for all, by the will of Christ. For the Church is the Body of Christ, and those who are ordained to act *in persona Christi*, "in the person of Christ," exercise headship in the Body, the Church. Paradoxically, the scandal of clergy sexual abuse, the manifest failures of many bishops to deal effectively with this crisis, and the justified anger this evoked among millions of faithful Catholics, demonstrated just how deep the Catholic memory of "headship" in fact is, even after decades of role-confusion.

That, however, is to take us in a different direction, toward a set of issues to be addressed later.

All ecumenical Councils have been followed by periods of turmoil—a good human reason, perhaps, why there have only been twenty-one such exercises in almost 2,000 years of Catholic history. In the inevitable turmoil following Vatican II, two things intersected: the Council's failure to address adequately the renewal of the priesthood, and misunderstandings of the new emphasis on "lay vocation." The net result was a serious crisis in priestly identity. Were ordained priests simply facilitators of the "ministries" of others—men who "empower others to exercise their gifts," as the post-conciliar jargon had it? If so, what is the point of celibacy? Indeed, if so, what is the point of ordination? The mass exodus from the priesthood in the two decades following the Council—46,000 priests abandoned their ministry around the world, the largest such defection since the sixteenth century Reformation—and the steep decline in U.S. seminary enrollment after the Council ended in December 1965 were the most obvious manifestations of this crisis of priestly identity.

From the beginning of his pontificate, in 1978, Pope John Paul II devoted considerable energies to addressing the crisis. Every Holy Thursday, when the Catholic Church traditionally commemorates the institution of the ordained priesthood by Christ at the Last Supper, the Pope wrote a lengthy letter to all the world's priests, addressing one or another facet of their unique vocation. John Paul repeatedly brought up the crisis of priestly identity and the reform of the priesthood in his discussions with, and addresses to, the bishops who came to Rome (as every bishop must) for their quinquennial meetings with the Pope and the Roman Curia. In 1990, the world Synod of Bishops spent a month debating the reform of seminaries and priestly formation. Two years later, on March 25, 1992, John Paul II completed the Synod's work with the apostolic exhortation *Pastores Dabo Vobis* [I Shall Give You Shepherds]. Quite probably the longest papal document in history, *Pastores*

Dabo Vobis explored the crisis of priestly identity, the renewal of priestly life, and the reform of seminaries in detail. The Pope's own heroic ideal of the priesthood, self-evidently lived out in his own life, has been a magnet attracting young men to similar lives of heroic virtue in the priesthood.

John Paul II's efforts were not without effect. That effect is evident in some seminaries today among younger priests formed in the image of John Paul II's pontificate, and among older priests who found their unique vocations reinvigorated by the Pope's teaching and example. But a tremendous amount of damage had been done to priestly identity in the two decades after Vatican II. That damage was manifest in defections from the priesthood, in a breakdown in clerical discipline, and in seminaries that failed to form men in any exercise of chastity, much less celibate chastity. The crisis of clergy sexual abuse brought that damage to public attention in an unmistakable way.

Priests who believe themselves to be what the Catholic Church teaches they are—living icons of the eternal priesthood of Jesus Christ—simply do not behave the way sexual predators behave. The crisis of priestly identity and the breakdown of clerical discipline that accompanied it have come at a very steep price.

A CRISIS OF EPISCOPAL LEADERSHIP

Why did the revelations of clerical sexual abuse in the first months of 2002 cause such a firestorm of anger, not only among the Church's habitual critics and enemies, but among Catholics?

Despite the confusions of recent decades, Catholics in America still esteem the priesthood. Sexual abuse by anyone is contemptible; still, adults know how widespread sexual abuse is in our society. Catholics, however, still rightly hold their priests to a higher standard of behavior. Then there was the fact that many of the allegations involved the sexual abuse of minors. While any form of sexual abuse is odious, the abuse of minors and children is particularly loathsome.

The deepest angers of Catholics, however, have been reserved for bishops: for bishops who seem to have done little or nothing to address the problem of clergy sexual abuse; for bishops whose most extensive efforts have seemed directed at keeping these problems out of the public eye; and for bishops who evidently did little to heal the personal and familial wounds caused by recklessly irresponsible priests. Given strong, even adequate, episcopal leadership—leadership willing to face facts and undertake essential reforms—the crisis of sexual abuse by priests need not have become the greatest crisis in the history of the Catholic Church in the United States. It became that because of the bishops' failure to lead.

How this failure happened will be discussed in detail below. The crucial point now is that these failures of leadership, like the failures manifest by clerical sexual predators, are also the result of a crisis of identity—in this case, the identity of the local bishop.

Scholars of the ancient world find no parallels to the Christian "bishop" among the leadership-types of antiquity. As they emerged in the first centuries of Christian history, bishops were authoritative teachers, sacral personalities who made possible the Church's worship, and governors who ruled by the authority of Christ—all at the same time. The Catholic bishop today must also teach, sanctify, and govern the local Church committed to his care. It is an awesome responsibility, for the bishop must answer to Christ, the Good Shepherd, for the well-being of the flock entrusted to him.

This point was emphasized by the Second Vatican Council, which made clear that the local bishop, in communion with the Bishop of Rome, the Successor of Peter, has real authority: He is not simply a local branch manager, executing orders devised "at the top." Yet many Catholic bishops today have taken an essentially managerial approach to their responsibilities. Some see their first responsibility as "keeping everyone in play" in a time of confusion and turmoil in the Church. Too many bishops in the United States seem to see themselves as men whose primary tasks are administrative and bureaucratic, rather than evangelical, pastoral, and catechetical; it is the rare diocesan bishop in the United States who devotes a fraction of the time he devotes to management to study, writing, preaching, or teaching. No one doubts that a bishop, whose responsibilities can include the management of a multimillion dollar non-profit organization, has serious administrative duties. But when "governing" is misunderstood on the model of discussion-group facilitation, or when governing trumps teaching and sanctifying in the local bishop's priorities, something is seriously awry. The results of that default—in self-understanding, and in true episcopal leadership—are now all too painfully clear.

The failures of episcopal leadership that turned a significant and urgent problem of clerical sexual abuse into a full-blown crisis touched all three of the bishop's classic roles, that is, as men who are to teach, govern, and sanctify. Too many bishops have manifestly failed to remind their priests and teach their people of some essential truths about the Catholic priesthood, and the relationship of that priesthood to celibate chastity. Too many bishops have failed to ensure that those truths were effectively taught in seminaries. Too many bishops have failed to move swiftly and decisively to see that clerical sexual predators are no longer a danger to the Church. Too many bishops have failed to act as pastors to the victims of clerical sexual abuse, and as agents of repentance and reconciliation in their local churches.

Too many bishops, in a word, have reacted to the multiple problems posed by the meltdown of priestly discipline and the subsequent outbreak of clerical sexual abuse as managers, not as apostles.

That is one of the primary reasons why Catholics were outraged in the first half of 2002. That is why a serious problem became a crisis.

A CRISIS OF DISCIPLESHIP

The crisis is also, and most fundamentally, a crisis of discipleship.

Because every Christian is baptized "into Christ," every Christian has a vocational responsibility to make Christ present in the world. Although that vocational responsibility is lived out in many different ways, every Christian vocation begins with baptism and with the baptismal responsibility to conform one's life to Christ.

Priests who are sexual predators behave in wicked ways because of a defective concept of the priesthood and an inadequate priestly formation. Even more fundamentally, though, clergy sexual abuse is the result of inadequate conversion to Christ. People who are truly living a new life in Christ do not treat others as objects of sexual manipulation. Before he is a Catholic priest, a man is a Christian disciple. If his discipleship is radically deficient, his priesthood will be distorted, too.

Bishops who cannot lead effectively are, in many instances, men who have absorbed a deficient understanding of the episcopate. Even more fundamentally, though, bishops who fail to teach, sanctify, and govern—bishops who fail to make manifest in their own ministry the living presence to the Church of Christ, the Good Shepherd—are men who have been inadequately converted to Christ.

Every Christian is called to be a saint. Indeed, "saints" are what every Christian must become if we are to enjoy eternal life with God. It takes a special kind of person to be able to live with God forever—it takes saints. When the Church recognizes someone publicly as a "saint," the Church is bearing witness to the truth that, in this world, a man or woman was so completely configured to Christ that this life of "heroic virtue" (in the technical language of saint-recognizing) is now continued in heaven, in joyful communion within the light and love of God.

Every Christian fails on the road to sanctity. Some of us fail often, and many of us fail grievously. In each case, the failure is one of discipleship. Men and women who have truly encountered the Risen Christ in the transforming experience of conversion—an experience that can take a lifetime—live different kinds of lives: They lead the life of a *disciple*. No one expects priests and bishops to be perfect. Like every other Christian, priests and bishops must face the "mystery of evil" at work in the world, as Pope John Paul II reminded priests in his Holy Thursday 2002 letter. Confronting that evil, priests and bishops will stumble and fall. That is why every priest and every bishop is expected to have a spiritual director and confessor.

Yet, recognizing that priests and bishops are "earthen vessels" [*2 Corinthians* 4.7] to whom the sacramental treasures of Christ have been committed is not the end of the matter. It is, in fact, only the beginning. Everyone can and should expect that men have been adequately converted to Christ before they are called by the Church to be priests or bishops. Everyone can and should expect that priests and bishops have made a fundamental, irrevocable, and life-transforming gift of their lives to Christ, in whom they have placed all their hope. And everyone can and should expect that no one will be called to the priesthood or the episcopate who is not willing to bear full public witness to that commitment to Christ, in and out of season, no matter what the difficulties.

By bearing that kind of witness, regardless of the cost, the priest and the bishop lift up and ennoble the vocations of every other member of the Church. That is not "clericalism." That is the truth that has formed the priesthood and the episcopate since New Testament times. That is the truth that must guide the reforms that are now blindingly necessary because of the two-edged crisis of clergy sexual abuse and episcopal leadership failure.

The crisis is a crisis of discipleship. The answer to the crisis is deeper fidelity.

By everyone.

CHAPTER TWO

WHAT THE
CRISIS IS NOT

T O FIX WHAT IS BROKEN in the Catholic Church in the United States requires a clear understanding of what the current crisis is *not*, as well as a clear understanding of what it is.

As the crisis broke into public attention in the first half of 2002, numerous misunderstandings quickly got into play, in reporting and commentary on the situation and in public discussion. Some of these misunderstandings were due to the lack of comprehensive data on clergy sexual abuse. Some were due to reportorial sloppiness. Some were the result of the thirty-year-old American tendency to read any institutional scandal through the prism of Watergate-style political warfare, with its vocabulary of "conspiracy," "cover-up," "crisis-management," "spin," and so forth. And some of the misunderstandings were generated by activists who unabashedly used the crisis to advance various agendas—a practice aptly described by one keen observer as "ideological joyriding."

What were these misunderstandings?

It was said, for example, that the crisis was a crisis of celibacy. It was not.

It was said that the crisis was due to the Catholic Church's "authoritarian" structures. But the Catholic Church's structure is not "authoritarian."

Some activists charged that the crisis grew out of a failure to "implement Vatican II fully," code for the *de facto* transformation of Catholicism into another liberal Protestant denomination. How this would have prevented the two-edged crisis of clerical sexual abuse and episcopal leadership failure was not self-evidently clear, not least because liberal Protestant denominations have their own serious problems of clergy sexual abuse.

Especially in its early months, the crisis was frequently described in the press as a "pedophilia crisis" or "crisis of child sexual abuse." The available data, however, suggest that classic pedophiles are as rare among Catholic priests as in the general population, and that the primary form of sexual abuse by Catholic clergy in recent decades has been the homosexual molestation of teenagers and young men.

It was frequently suggested, if not openly asserted, that

clerical sexual abuse is ongoing and widespread, although there is no reliable data to support this claim.

Traditionalist Catholics, some American Catholic churchmen, and more than a few Roman officials claimed that the crisis was created by the mass media—a "feeding frenzy," as one U.S. cardinal put it. Yet even a feeding frenzy requires something to feed on.

Catholic dissidents frequently and loudly proclaimed the crisis the product of the Catholic Church's inhumane, repressive sexual ethic. Yet the counter-claim—that the crisis of clerical sexual abuse was one grim by-product of the general breakdown of sexual morality in society—was at least as plausible a hypothesis, given that clerical sexual predators had committed acts the Catholic Church flatly condemns.

A brief examination of each of these misunderstandings should help clarify just what the crisis is, as well as what it is not.

CELIBACY

At the most basic, empirical level, the claim that the crisis was caused by celibacy made no sense, for the crisis was self-evidently triggered, not by faithful celibates, but by men who had failed to live the celibate vows they had made. To blame the crisis of sexual abuse on celibacy is about as plausible as blaming adultery on the marriage vow, or blaming treason on the Pledge of Allegiance. It just doesn't parse.

The confusions on this front went much deeper than the empirical, however.

It is not easy to understand, much less appreciate, a lifelong commitment to celibate chastity in a culture that regards sex as another contact sport: a culture of "self-expression" in which sexual pleasure is a "right" and the mastery of one's sexual desires is often deemed "repression." Read through the lens of the sexual revolution, celibacy is peculiar at best and pathological at worst. Thus the connection was quickly made between the Catholic Church's practice of priestly celibacy and the crisis of clergy sexual abuse. Celibates, it was suggested, were especially prone to sexual predation because they were maladjusted psychologically and required some form of release, however perverse, for their sexual tensions.

The data simply do not support these claims. Celibates do not dominate the national registry of sex offenders. Sexual abuse and sexual harassment are frequently committed by married men. A man given to sexual predation is unlikely to be restrained by marriage. The related suggestions that celibacy is the primary problem in the crisis of sexual abuse, and that a married clergy would be less given to sexual abuse, also demean marriage. The implication is that marriage is a crime-prevention program, not a covenant of mutual love and self-giving.

Grappling with the Catholic understanding of celibacy also means recognizing that Catholicism, like all great religious traditions, is not a simple business. It takes a serious effort to get inside the Catholic Church's self-understanding and see how the pieces of the mosaic fit together. That kind of effort is especially important when dealing with so countercultural a Catholic practice as priestly celibacy. Unless the effort is made, however, the terrible simplifiers win the day and both history and theology get distorted in the process. That is what happened here.

It was often said during the break-out of the crisis that celibacy is merely a "discipline" with no innate connection to the priesthood. Moreover, one frequently heard, mandatory clerical celibacy was a relatively late development in Catholic history. What was made binding throughout the western Church in the twelfth century could be changed by the Church in the twenty-first century, in a return to the more ancient practice of a married clergy.

Both the theology and the history were seriously awry on these points. The situation is much more complicated, and thus much more interesting.

In the *Letter to the Ephesians*, Saint Paul describes the relationship of Christ, the eternal high priest, to his Church as the relationship of a spouse to a beloved bride: Christ the redeemer gives himself to his spouse freely, unreservedly, faithfully, and unto death. If a Catholic priest is not a religious bureaucrat who conducts certain kinds of churchly business, but rather an icon—a living re-presentation—of the eternal priesthood of Jesus Christ, then the priest's relationship to his bride, the Church, should be like Christ's—the priest is to give himself to the Church freely, unreservedly, faithfully, and unto death. And he must be *seen* to be doing so. His commitment to his bride must be visible in his way of life, as well as in his heart and soul.

That is why the Catholic Church places such a high value on celibacy. Chaste celibate love for the Church is another "icon" of Christ's presence to his people. The Christ whom the priest makes present through his sacramental ministry at the altar and in the confessional is acting, not simply in the name of Christ, but in the *person* of Christ. According to ancient Catholic usage, he is "another Christ," an *alter Christus*, whose complete gift of self to the Church is an integral part of his priestly persona. Celibacy is thus not "extrinsic" to the Catholic priesthood, a mere matter of ecclesiastical discipline. There is an intimate, personal, iconic relationship between celibacy and priesthood.

The history of clerical celibacy bears this out. Recent historical studies have demonstrated that, when the Second Lateran Council made clerical celibacy legally binding for the entire western Church in 1129, its decision was the end-point of a lengthy period of development and a ratification of what had long been understood to be the norm for priests. It was not, primarily, a matter of Lateran II trying to address certain medieval issues of property-law and inheritance. A law, whether civil or ecclesiastical, is often the last step in the crystallization of a community's convictions on a subject. According to contemporary scholars, that is what happened with

Lateran II's legislation on celibacy in 1129. The law of clerical celibacy adopted in the twelfth century gave legal form to a longstanding practice that had been promoted and defended as an important facet of priestly life for centuries. The practice of priestly celibacy in fact goes back to the Church's origins. It was not an invention of the Middle Ages.

Yes, the western Church ordained married men to the priesthood in the first millennium, as the eastern-rite Catholic Churches and the Orthodox Church ordain married men as priests today. At the same time, however, the western Church in the first millennium typically required those married men, with the consent of their wives, to refrain from "using the rights of marriage" after their priestly ordination, in order to express through continence the iconography of the priest's unique relationship to the Church as his bride. When the history is read like this, things look different today. It was not the western Church that went off on a tangent by making celibacy a general requirement in the twelfth century. It was the eastern churches that continued to ordain married men without a promise of sexual abstinence, that diverted from the main trajectory of development (a point further underscored by the fact that the eastern churches only ordain celibates to the fullness of the priesthood, the episcopate). That, at least, is what the contemporary scholarship suggests.

A tangled historical and theological question like this cannot be easily settled. The fact that there are faithful, effective married priests in the Catholic Church (either eastern-rite priests, or converts from Anglicanism or Lutheranism) certainly must be part of any discussion of priesthood and celibacy today. What any serious person can grasp, however, is that celibacy for the Catholic Church is essentially something positive, not negative. It is the embodiment, in a self-sacrificial way of life, of a complete gift of self to Christ and the Church. Celibacy tells us what a man is for, not what he's against.

The celibate, who freely chooses not to do something very good—marry—also ennobles marriage. The sacrifice of a good reminds us just how good something is. To understand celibacy undertaken "for the Kingdom" as a deprecation of marriage and of sexual love is to misunderstand celibacy, marriage, sexual love, and the Kingdom of God.

An "Authoritarian" Church?

Both secular commentators and Catholic dissenters charged that the crisis of clergy sexual abuse and episcopal leadership failure was due to the "authoritarian" structures of the Catholic Church. The problem with this argument is that the Catholic Church is not an authoritarian institution, nor are its leaders authoritarians.

An "authoritarian" is someone who makes someone else do something purely as a matter of willfulness: You do this because *I* say so. An authoritarian does not give reasons for his or her decisions or commands. Similarly, the subjects of an authoritarian ruler have nothing to say about what they're being commanded to do. Indeed, there are no "subjects" of a genuinely authoritarian regime, only "objects" to be manipulated at will by the ruler.

That is not the way the Catholic Church works.

The Catholic Church believes that it has a "form" or structure given to it by Christ. That structure is composed in part of truths: truths about God, truths about human beings, truths about our relationship to God and God's relationship to us. The pastoral authorities of the Church—the college of bishops, with and under the headship of the Bishop of Rome—are the custodians of this *authoritative* tradition, which binds the Church, including popes and bishops, across the centuries. Popes and bishops do not make things up as they go along. Doctrine is not a matter of papal or episcopal whim or willfulness. Popes and bishops are the servants, not the masters, of the tradition—the truths—that make the Church what it is. Thus the pope and the bishops are *authoritative teachers*, not authoritarian despots.

Moreover, the Catholic Church believes that the truths it has been given by Christ free us as well as bind us. They are liberating truths. To accept the Church's teaching as authoritative and binding is only a "restriction" on my freedom if I imagine freedom to be the unbridled exercise of my imagination and will. (And in that case, I have chained myself to my own willfulness.) If freedom has something to do with learning to choose what is genuinely good, for myself and for others, then the truth about what's good for me and for others isn't a restriction. It's a means of liberation. The opposite of "authoritarian" isn't "autonomous" or "willful." The opposite of "authoritarian" is *authoritative*.

The Catholic crisis that broke into public view in early 2002 does, in fact, have a lot to do with the way authority is and isn't exercised in the Church. It certainly had a lot to do with abysmal failures by some of the Church's pastoral leaders—its bishops—to exercise the authority that is theirs. The crisis should also raise the question of whether the ways in which the bishops of the United States have functioned corporately in recent decades have impeded their individual capacities to be authoritative teachers and true heads of their local churches. These are questions to be explored later.

But the crisis did not have anything to do with the fact that the Catholic Church believes that it is formed and bound by an authoritative tradition. If anything, the opposite is the case. The crisis was caused in no small part by confusions and ambiguities about the truths that make the Church what it is, confusions and ambiguities too prevalent among the Church's priests and bishops.

A Failure to Implement Vatican II?

Almost four decades after the Second Vatican Council concluded its epic work, an aging, intellectually sterile, and numerically shrinking cadre of Catholic dissidents continues to insist that every problem in the Catholic Church today is caused by a failure to implement the Council's teaching and "spirit." This failure is typically described as a failure to "democratize" the Church, or to "share authority." Those to be "empowered," in what the dissidents wrongly imagine to be "reform," are typically intellectuals or activists.

It seems of little consequence to those who have chanted this mantra of democratization and power-sharing for more than thirty-five years that Vatican II solemnly reaffirmed the supreme authority of the pope as chief pastor of the Church, or that the Council taught that local bishops, in communion with the Bishop of Rome, enjoy full ecclesial authority. The vocabulary of "empowerment" and "power-sharing" also fudges the full and complex truth of the Council's teaching on the priesthood of all the baptized and the priesthood of the Church's ordained ministers. For while Vatican II affirmed the ancient truth that all the baptized share in the priesthood of Christ and exercise that common priesthood in prayer, the Council also affirmed the unique character of the ordained priesthood as being different in kind, not simply in degree, from the priestly character of the laity. Dissidents rarely if ever mention the Council's teaching that celibacy has an important relationship to priesthood. For those convinced that the "spirit of Vatican II" requires the Catholic Church to become another American "denomination" in its approach to doctrine and in its structures of authority and responsibility, what Vatican II actually taught seems of little consequence.

The sixteen documents of Vatican II can, of course, be read in different ways within the boundaries of Catholic orthodoxy. The history of the Council, its intentions and tensions, is just now being written. The Catholic Church will be debating the meaning of Vatican II for decades, perhaps centuries. That is perfectly understandable, and perfectly acceptable. Ecumenical councils always take decades, even centuries, to digest.

What is neither understandable nor acceptable is the dissidents' suggestion that Catholicism should follow the self-destructive path charted by liberal Protestant denominations that have been hemorrhaging congregants for decades. Christian communities that deconstruct themselves doctrinally and morally have been failing dramatically since the Second World War, to the point where liberal Protestantism will be a mere fraction of world Protestant Christianity by the middle of the twenty-first century. If good fences make good neighbors, as poet Robert Frost suggested, clear doctrinal and moral boundaries seem to make for vibrant Christian communities. The answer to the two-edged crisis of clerical sexual abuse and inert episcopal leadership cannot be found in making Catholicism's boundaries so porous that no one is certain what constitutes fidelity or infidelity. On the contrary, it is precisely such porousness that has helped create the current crisis.

The crisis has everything to do with the authentic implementation of Vatican II, and with the failure of the Church's leadership to do just that. But what the dissidents mean by the implementation of Vatican II is more accurately described as the demolition of Catholicism.

A "PEDOPHILIA CRISIS"?

The sexual molestation of young children is the most revolting aspect of the broader problem of clergy sexual abuse—as the failure of bishops to deal effectively with this dimension of the crisis is one of the most incomprehensible aspects of the broader problem of the failure of episcopal leadership. Because the Archdiocese of Boston was the first focus of media attention in the crisis, and because two Boston abusers, John Geoghan and Paul Shanley, sexually molested children (a practice Shanley advocated in the North American Man-Boy Love Association, one of whose mottos is "Eight is too late"), the crisis was quickly labeled a "pedophila" crisis or "crisis of child sexual abuse." Given the Geoghan and Shanley cases, this was understandable. As further evidence of the breadth of the crisis of clerical sexual abuse came to light, though, it also became clear that the description was inaccurate.

Pedophile priests—in the classic sense of men who habitually abuse prepubescent children—are not the majority of clerical sexual abusers; they are, in fact, a small minority of malfeasant clergy, although they are arguably the most loathsome form of the clerical sexual predator. That the shorthand of a "pedophilia crisis" was still being used in the *Washington*

Post, by Reuters news service, and by other media outlets months after even gay activists were conceding that the overwhelming majority of the abuses reported involved homosexual men molesting teenage boys or young males suggested that the moniker "pedophila crisis" served agendas other than factual accuracy. Were the crisis of clerical sexual abuse to be described accurately—as a crisis whose principle manifestation was homosexual molestation—other questions about gay culture might well be raised. This, evidently, some did not wish to do, including dissident Catholic moral theologians.

A simple test is a virtually infallible indicator of whether a person or institution is capable of understanding the current crisis and is willing to address it at its roots. It matters not whether the person is Catholic on non-Catholic, bishop, priest, or layman; it matters not whether the institutions is a newspaper, newsmagazine, television program, or talk show. Does that person or institution describe the demographics of clergy sexual abuse accurately, avoiding the all-purpose label, "pedophilia crisis"? If they do not, there are other agendas in play.

A MEDIA-CREATED CRISIS?

As the crisis unfolded in the first half of 2002, Vatican officials, a few American churchmen, and some Catholic activists of a traditionalist bent were suggesting that the problem of sexual abuse, while real and serious, had been manufactured into a public crisis by an overwrought American media. Some of these critics suggested that the press was indulging its post-Watergate addiction to institutional scandal, and had simply turned its guns from the beaten-dead horse of the Enron Corporation to the Catholic Church. Others went farther, suggesting that the press were determined to bring down the one institution in the United States that refused to buckle to political correctness in matters of abortion, euthanasia, cloning, stem-cell research, and "gay marriage." This latter charge was frequently heard with reference to the *Boston Globe*, which for years had published a wide variety of anti-Catholic columnists (some of them, like veteran Catholic dissident James Carroll, ex-priests). When the *Globe* broke the Geoghan and Shanley stories and followed those up with an editorial call for the resignation of Boston's archbishop, Cardinal Bernard F. Law, more than a few Catholics (including some who were highly critical of Cardinal Law's handling of the crisis) thought it possible to connect the dots between the *Globe's* attitude toward the Church over the past twenty years and its present position on the crisis. One also looked long and hard on the editorial and op-ed pages of the *New York Times* for anything other than the rawest attacks on Catholic doctrine and practice, from dissident Catholics as well as the *Times'* regular stable of lifestyle-libertine columnists.

Responsible reporters, columnists, and editors admit that there were problems with coverage of the crisis in the first half of 2002. At the beginning, press coverage created the impression that pedophile John Geoghan was the typical clerical sexual predator, when in fact he was not only atypical among priests but abnormal among sexual abusers who had undergone extensive therapy. This, in turn, led to fears that the crisis of clergy sexual abuse was ongoing, massive in scope, and out of control, when, in fact, few instances of abuse from the 1990s came to light. Thus the media generally missed the story of those reforms in seminary recruitment and training, and in diocesan clergy personnel policies, that seem to have proven effective in preventing sexual abuse. At the same time, the early coverage of Geoghan, and of the Boston archdiocese's efforts to settle with his victims privately, fed a panic atmosphere in some Catholic quarters about the "safety of the children."

As indicated previously, the press was late, and then reluctant, to acknowledge the truth embedded in its own reporting, that homosexual molestation of teenagers and young men was the most prevalent form of clerical sexual abuse. To take but one example, for two weeks in April one reporter for a prominent national daily repeatedly tried and failed to get this phrase past her editors: "Those who raise the issue of homosexuality in connection with the scandals note that very few of the abuse victims have been female." When the facts of the matter could no longer be avoided, the pendulum sometimes swung in the other direction, with reporters and columnists blithely citing the exaggerated estimates of a 30 to 50 percent gay Catholic clergy bruited by former Cleveland seminary rector, Father Donald Cozzens. (The most knowledgeable social scientist studying these questions, Philip Jenkins of Pennsylvania State University, argues that "men with gay inclinations" are found in the priesthood in the United States at a rate substantially higher than in the average male population, but not in the range of Father Cozzens's figures.)

No one could blame reporters for seeking the opinions of Catholic dissidents on the crisis; they, too, are part of the story. Still, reportorial probes into the possibility that the crisis had roots in the Catholic culture of dissent were rare. So were explorations of how the infatuation of bishops and seminary faculties with the claims of psychological and psychiatric therapists had contributed to the crisis. Some of the therapists who were arguably responsible for the recycling of clerical sexual predators were themselves frequently quoted as authorities; evidently, their past performance was deemed irrelevant, so long as they now hewed to the line that the Church's commitment to celibacy and its critique of the sexual revolution were at fault in the current crisis.

Criticism of Pope John Paul II's "silence" by reporters, editorial writers, and columnists seemed strained. The Pope had in fact spoken and written extensively about the reform of the priesthood for twenty-three years. Moreover, it made no sense to expect that the Pope could function as a kind of super-personnel manager for every Catholic diocese in the world. The media also created story-lines by which it then judged the Church's performance. To take but one example: it was the press which first decided that "zero tolerance" was *the* issue at the American cardinals' meeting in Rome on April 22–23, 2002, and then judged the cardinals' performance by a standard that the press itself had designed. That several cardinals fell into this trap surely says something about their competence, but it does not change the essential facts. In this instance and others (and not unlike the way the media functions in big-time political or corporate scandals), reporters appoint themselves prosecutor, jury, judge, and appeals court, passing judgment on laws they themselves have promulgated.

That all being said, it was a serious mistake for some Catholic leaders and Catholic traditionalists to argue that the crisis was created by a media feeding frenzy. It was not. The crisis was, and is, the Church's crisis. Even if much of the media tended to read the crisis through typical secular and political filters, two indisputable facts remained: clergy sexual abuse was a serious problem in the Catholic Church for decades; many bishops did not recognize the problem, or recognizing it, failed to act on both the problem and its sources. When those two facts intersected, the facts produced a crisis. The media did not produce the crisis.

Moreover, as more than one Catholic highly critical of the bishops' performance (and, needless to say, of clergy sexual predation) pointed out, the Church owes the press a debt of gratitude. Because of the press, some sexual predators have been arrested and jailed. Because of the press, the authorities were able to locate predators like Paul Shanley and former Dallas priest Rudy Kos before they could do any more damage to young minds and souls; in both instances, Church leaders had failed to protect either the Church or society. Because of the press, the Catholic Church has been forced to recognize that it is in more trouble than its leaders and people might have imagined. Whether that blunt recognition is taken to the next level—whether it extends to a similarly blunt recognition of the roots of the crisis and a committed grappling with the thoroughgoing reforms necessary to turn a crisis into an opportunity for renewal—remains to be seen. That, no one will know for years. But even the most ardent Catholic must freely concede this: It is very unlikely that the Catholic Church in the United States would be asking these questions without the goad of the press. And for that Catholics should be grateful. In all of this, Catholics must believe God's saving purposes are somehow being worked out. If God could work through the Assyrians in the Old Testament, God can certainly work through the *New York Times* and the *Boston Globe* today, whether the *Times* and the *Globe* realize what's happening or not.

This is not a media crisis. It is a Catholic crisis—a crisis of fidelity. It certainly seemed like a media feeding frenzy at times. It is delusional and self-destructive for Catholics to believe that that sums up the matter.

Is the Catholic
Sexual Ethic at Fault?

Secular critics and Catholic dissidents alike argued that the crisis was the by-product of what they imagined to be the Church's hoary, "medieval" sexual ethic. On this view, there was a direct line between the 1968 encyclical *Humanae Vitae*, which reaffirmed the Catholic Church's teaching that natural family planning is the morally appropriate way to regulate births, and the crisis of clergy sexual abuse. The critics and the dissidents were right. But not in the way they imagined.

That, however, is a story for the next chapter.

As with the charge that the crisis was caused by celibacy, the claim that the Church's sexual ethic was the root cause of the crisis missed an obvious fact: Sexual abusers are manifestly and unmistakably *not* living the Church's sexual ethic. On the contrary, they are doing what the Catholic Church *condemns*. More than one Vatican official, puzzled at the drumbeat of reportorial inquiries in March 2002 about "the Pope's attitude toward clergy sexual abuse," must have been tempted to reply, simply, "He's very much against it." What else could he be? What else could the Church be?

As articulated by Pope John Paul II in his groundbreaking "theology of the body," the Catholic sexual ethic holds that sexual love is a matter of self-giving, not self-assertion—as indeed all genuine love is a matter of self-gift, not self-assertion. Moreover, the Catholic Church teaches that to give oneself to another through sexual love within the bond of faithful and fruitful marriage is an icon of the interior life of God himself—for God the Holy Trinity is a community of radical self-giving and receptivity. Journalists tend to reduce the Catholic sexual ethic to prohibitions on contraception and homosexual activity without asking about the affirmations that undergird those prohibitions. Most Catholics have never heard of John Paul II's "theology of the body," and Catholic dissidents tend to dismiss it because it leads to conclusions about contraception, premarital sex, and homosexuality they cannot tolerate. The fact, though, is that the Catholic Church has a higher view of human sexuality than the editors of *Playboy* or *Cosmopolitan*. The Catholic Church teaches that our sexuality teaches us deep truths about ourselves—and about God. Neither Hugh Hefner nor Helen Gurley Brown would dare make such a claim.

If there is a failure here, and there clearly is, it is the failure of the Church's pastors in the United States (and elsewhere) to teach the Church's sexual ethic as an ethic that affirms and celebrates the gift of sexual love. Popular impressions notwithstanding, Catholics in America are not regularly dunned with sermons about the evils of certain sexual practices. The truth of the matter is that most Catholics in the United States could count on one hand the number of sermons on sexual morality that they've heard in the last decade. Some could count on one finger.

This, in turn, suggests another dimension of the crisis: The

Catholic Church in the United States has not learned to be comfortably countercultural in teaching its sexual ethic and in calling the people of the Church to the adventure of fidelity. Catholics are, *very* occasionally, urged to walk the walk of chaste sexual love as the Catholic Church understands it. Catholic bishops and priests almost never talk the talk of the Church's sexual ethic in persuasive, compelling ways that see and then raise the stakes posed by the sexual revolution. It can be done. A few scholars and an increasing number of young Catholic couples who have learned the "theology of the body" in Catholic renewal movements can, and do, talk the talk. When they do, skeptical secularists and committed feminists find in the "theology of the body" a genuine contribution to human thought and a defense of the moral foundations of civilization, not a repressive rejection of sex. Perhaps the Church, in the wake of this crisis, can begin talking the talk to itself about these matters.

CHAPTER THREE

HOW THE
CRISIS HAPPENED

MODERN BIBLICAL SCHOLARSHIP confirms the classic Catholic view that the New Testament was the
product of the primitive Christian Church. The books of the
New Testament were not dictated by God to holy scribes,
word by word. Rather, these writings emerged from early
Christian communities whose experiences of discipleship and
its dilemmas shaped their reception of God's word. Research
has also shown that the twenty-seven books of the New Testament were not the only Christian literature written during
the first Christian century; other gospels, letters, and apoca-
lyptic books abound. It was an inspired act of the Church—a
self-defining act, if you will—to determine that *these* twenty-

seven books, rather than others, would be in the canon of sacred scripture. As the Church made those decisions under the guidance of the Holy Spirit, the Church was clarifying essential truths of salvation history for herself and for future generations. From the beginning, the Church's scripture was meant to instruct as well as to record.

That the New Testament is very much the "Church's book" makes it all the more striking that all four gospel accounts of the life of Christ record the betrayal of Judas Iscariot. One of the Twelve, the men closest to Christ, betrayed Jesus to enemies who then put him to death. A man personally chosen by Christ for intimate friendship and for a heroic mission betrayed him. The Gospel of Luke even suggests that Judas participated in the institution of the Eucharist at the Last Supper—which, according to ancient Catholic tradition, would make Judas the first priest to betray Christ.

Assembling the New Testament, the early Church could have elided over the story of Judas's betrayal, just as it could have skipped lightly over the story of Peter's denial and the other apostles' flight from the Garden of Gethsemane after the arrest of Jesus. That the Church resolutely insisted on including these tales of betrayal by the Lord's first chosen ones tells us something about the early Church, and something about the Church at all times.

It tells us that betrayal has been part of the Christian story from the beginning, a fact from which early Christians evidently did not flinch. Just as important as its honesty about its black sheep, however, was the early Church's recognition that betrayal is *not* the story line of the Church. Fidelity is. That is the story told in the *Acts of the Apostles*—the story of those who lived the truth of their apostolic and priestly vocations and took the Gospel "to the end of the earth" [*Acts* 1.8]. Judas is mentioned in *Acts*, prior to the selection of Matthias, his replacement in the Twelve, but treason is not the main story line in *Acts*. Faithful witness, often unto death, is the story.

What would have happened if the apostles (who were, according to Catholic tradition, the Church's first priests and bishops) had become completely demoralized and paralyzed by the betrayal of their fellow apostle? What would have happened if the members of the early Church had been so scandalized by Judas's treason that they could not grasp how God always brings good out of evil?

Betrayal has been part of the Church's reality—and part of the reality of the priesthood and episcopate—from the beginning. Betrayal is not the last word in the Church's story, however. The men who fled from Gethsemane in a panic of fear were transformed by the Risen Christ and the Holy Spirit into men on fire, men who could not do anything else but witness to the truth of God's salvation in Christ, even when it cost them their lives. God can, does, and always will bring good out of evil, even an evil so great as the treacherous betrayal of God's Son.

Which is a good thing to remember while considering how the most recent betrayals of the priesthood and the episcopate—which are always betrayals of Christ—came about.

Why Now? Why This Way?

Over almost two millennia, the story of the priesthood and the episcopate in the Catholic Church can be read as a continuing tale of fidelity, betrayal, and reform—followed by fidelity, betrayal, and reform.

The eleventh century subservience of medieval bishops to their princes led to the reforms of Pope Gregory VII and the struggle between Church and Holy Roman Emperor over the appointment of bishops—a struggle with immense implications for the next millennium of European history. In one of the fiercest tracts of that time, *The Book of Gomorrah*, Peter Damian, later canonized as a saint and honored for his theological accomplishments as a Doctor of the Church, condemned clerical sodomy, demanded that Pope Leo IX take action against the decadent churchmen of the eleventh century, and argued that some sins render a man unfit for any future exercise of the ministry. The corruptions of the priesthood and the episcopate in the immediate pre-Reformation Church led to the reforms of the Council of Trent and a seminary system that served the Church well for more than 350 years. In each of these instances, and in the many others that could be cited, reform of the priesthood and the episcopate required a clear analysis of the causes of corruption, which varied from age to age—even as different forms of clerical perversity and episcopal malfeasance all sprang from inadequate conversion to Christ.

Why is the Catholic Church in the United States suffering a crisis of clerical sexual abuse and inadequate episcopal leadership now, in the first years of the twenty-first century? Why does so much of that abuse seem to cluster in a period between the early 1960s and the late 1980s?

The first six decades of the twentieth century were, arguably, a Golden Age for the Catholic priesthood in the United States; as one American bishop has put it, for a boy to aspire to the priesthood in the mid–twentieth century was to aspire to the highest calling imaginable. Priests were generously supported by their people. With rare exceptions in pockets of anti-Catholic bigotry, Catholic priests were respected members of society, men treated as heroes in popular culture. Seminaries and novitiates were full, and so were parish rectories and religious houses. What transformed a Golden Age into a period of confusion that produced the greatest clerical crisis in U.S. Catholic history?

Traditionalist Catholics tend to blame the Second Vatican Council: if not its teaching, then its relaxation of Church discipline. Dissident Catholics blame an alleged failure to live the "spirit of Vatican II." Both are right in that the uproar the Council unleashed in the Church eventually helped produce today's crisis. But every ecumenical council has produced an uproar in its wake. Why did *this* council, Vatican II, produce *this* kind of scandal and *this* kind of inadequate episcopal response to it?

As is often the case, timing was everything.

The Council, it is often said, urged the Church to "open its windows to the modern world." That is true enough. The more complete truth, however, is that the Council urged a two-way dialogue between the Church and modernity, in which the modern world would also be challenged to open its windows to the worlds of which it was a part, including the world of transcendent Truth and Love. Be that as it may, one of the most important things that many U.S. Catholic priests, bishops, nuns, theologians, and lay activists took away from Vatican II was the idea that the Church had to "open its windows to the modern world."

What these Catholic leaders failed to notice at the time— and what some Catholic leaders refuse to acknowledge today—is that the Catholic Church opened its windows just as the modern, western world was barreling into a dark tunnel full of poisonous fumes.

By the time the Church got its windows open in the mid-1960s there were all sorts of toxins in the air. In high culture, and especially in intellectual life, the bright hopes of "modernity" were being dashed on the rocks of irrationality, self-indulgence, fashionable despair, and contempt for any traditional authority. The mid-century's two premier philosophers—Martin Heidegger and Jean-Paul Sartre—had, it turned out, been supporters of two of the great butchers in a century of slaughter: Hitler for Heidegger, and Stalin for Sartre. Their political blindness presaged decades in which intellectuals, having abandoned the search for truth, fell into a quicksand pit of self-absorption, emerging to find themselves often allied to odious political causes. A dialogue about the future of humanism with intellectuals convinced that western civilization was fundamentally corrupt because of racism, imperialism, and misogyny was not going to be easy.

Some churchmen tried valiantly to redeem the promise of the Council's anticipated dialogue with modernity. The same Jean-Marie Lustiger who attended political science lectures at the Sorbonne in the 1950s with a Cambodian intellectual named Pol Pot would become an effective catechist in radically secular French intellectual circles, and later the Archbishop of Paris. Karol Wojtyła of Kraków, another young priest passionately interested in modern philosophy, led decades of dialogue with secular and agnostic Polish intellectuals, in a common effort to parse the true meaning of human freedom under communist tyranny; Wojtyła would bring the lessons of those dialogues to Rome as Pope John Paul II. But despite these and other examples of genuine conversation and exchange, the fact remained that the late 1960s were a very difficult time for a two-way conversation between an ancient religious tradition built on the foundation of what it understood to be truths-with-consequences for all humanity, and an intellectual world deeply skeptical that there was, in fact, any such thing as "truth."

Other key themes of contemporary culture made Catholicism's post-Vatican II encounter with modernity difficult—more difficult than perhaps some of the most optimistic bishops at the Council imagined. How could a Church formed by an authoritative tradition present itself in a culture that looked askance on any form of traditional authority, and especially religious authority? The label "authoritarian" quickly got applied to the Church, and stuck. In the 1960s, the Church also met an old enemy tarted up in modern guise: gnosticism, the ancient heresy which denied that the material world really counts for anything. For almost two millennia, the Catholic Church has insisted that stuff counts—that bread and water, oil and salt, and sexual love within the bond of marital fidelity could be transformed into sacramental encounters with God himself. Why? Because the ordinary stuff of this world is never as ordinary as it seems; it always points beyond itself to the extraordinary love of God for his creation. How could this kind of Church teach its message in a world that, for all its luxuriant materiality, seemed not to take the material world seriously, treating material things (including the human body) as mere toys for manipulation in an endless quest for self-expression and pleasure? Then there was the modern quest for freedom. How could a Church committed to the idea that freedom has everything to do with truth and goodness make its case in a culture in which freedom was broadly understood as license—"I did it *my* way"?

The basic problem—how to have a genuine dialogue with modernity that did not involve the Church choking on some of the modern world's most noxious fumes—was difficult enough. The difficulties were further compounded by the tremendous organizational shake-up the Catholic Church in the United States experienced just after Vatican II.

If any decade in the history of American Catholicism bears out the caricature of the Catholic Church as a kind of ecclesiastical army in which commands from the top are quickly transmitted down the chain of command and executed without question, it was the Catholic 1950s. The pent-up energies from that period of strict ecclesiastical discipline, plus the radical cultural environment of the 1960s, plus the Council's mandate for new forms of Church governance, made for a heady, even explosive, brew. The net result was a dramatic change in the atmosphere and self-discipline of the Catholic Church throughout the United States. The lifestyles of Catholic priests changed, and so did priests' attitudes toward bishops; confrontations with authority that were quite unimaginable in the late 1950s were quite commonplace by the late 1960s. Seminaries, which once vied with military academies as strictly run institutions for training highly disciplined professionals, were transformed within a half-decade and came to resemble university dormitories or fraternity houses. A rapid and large exodus from the active priesthood in the decades after Vatican II put a high institutional premium on keeping those who remained (as priests or seminarians) happy, which in turn reinforced the general loosening of clerical discipline.

These changes paralleled a rapid bureaucratization of U.S. Catholic life at every level from the local parish to the national bishops' conference. Those new offices were frequently filled by activists and intellectuals who, in the manner of all bureaucracies, created a self-perpetuating elite. In this case, it was an elite committed to the "spirit of Vatican II" and determined to advance an agenda of radical change through bureaucratic means when persuasion failed, or when the Vatican said "No." The Catholic Left's long march through the institutions of the Church had begun.

Then, and most urgently, there was the sexual revolution, a cultural explosion that had been brewing in the western world since the 1920s. The decadence of that era could not last, however, because the Great Depression put a high economic premium on maintaining the traditional family and the Second World War was not a congenial time for drastic social change. Fifteen years or so after the war, however, a sexual revolution that made the Flapper Era of the 1920s look comparatively tame broke out with full force throughout the western world. It was the heyday of Freudianism, and what earlier generations regarded as the self-mastery of sexual desires the high culture of the West now believed to be unhealthy "repression." The contraceptive pill seemed to promise pleasure without consequences in a safe, carefree sexual environment. Changing attitudes toward abortion, and ultimately legal change, contributed to the increasingly widespread notion that sex is simply a form of recreation, in which "anything goes" so long as "no one else gets hurt." Traditional sexual mores were in meltdown throughout society, and western culture became sex-saturated.

The Catholic intellectual encounter with modernity in the immediate aftermath of Vatican II led to important theological accomplishments. It also led to a period of serious doctrinal confusion, particularly in moral theology. A vibrant, growing community like the Catholic Church in the United States could not be run like the Church of the 1950s, out of the local bishop's back pocket and from his living room desk. But the explosion of bureaucracy in the Church after Vatican II, and dramatic changes in the way bishops understood their office, made it ever more difficult to maintain doctrinal cohesion and ecclesiastical discipline—problems exacerbated by what often seemed to be uncertain papal leadership during the fifteen-year pontificate of Pope Paul VI (1963–1978). And so it was that, when the sexual revolution hit the Catholic Church with the force of a hurricane, the Church was intellectually, organizationally, and spiritually ill-prepared for the blow.

The results are now obvious, in the crisis of clergy sexual abuse and its magnification by incompetent or malfeasant episcopal leadership. "The Sixties" did not "cause" the crisis, which is primarily the Church's responsibility. In the late 1960s, however, a culture of dissent took root in the Catholic Church in the United States, unmistakably influenced by the spirit of the times. In that culture of dissent, "fidelity" took on a new meaning—or, perhaps better, "fidelity" lost its true, ecclesial meaning. At precisely the same time, the crisis of clergy sexual abuse gathered such critical mass that it spilled over into the next two decades. The timing was not accidental. Neither was the relationship between clergy sexual abuse and the culture of dissent.

THE "TRUCE OF 1968"

The public controversy over Pope Paul VI's encyclical, *Humanae Vitae*, was perhaps the crucial moment in the formation of a culture of dissent that would influence the Catholic Church in the United States for the rest of the twentieth century.

Issued on July 25, 1968, *Humanae Vitae* reaffirmed the Catholic Church's teaching that using the natural rhythms of fertility as a means of family planning is the morally appropriate way to regulate births. The encyclical bitterly disappointed those who had hoped (and lobbied) for papal moral approval of the contraceptive pill; it enraged those theologians who had worked hard to make the "birth control" controversy the vehicle for dramatic changes in the way the Catholic Church thought and taught about moral issues in general. The resulting acrimony was fierce.

Public dissent from *Humanae Vitae* began even before the official text of the encyclical was made available. It was led, not by disappointed laity, but by priests, religious, and theologians, some of them men and women of considerable influence. One focal point of the dissent was the Archdiocese of Washington. Priests of the archdiocese joined the public dissent against the encyclical (which was intense at the Washington-based Catholic University of America) and, after several warnings, nineteen Washington priests were disciplined by the local archbishop, Cardinal Patrick O'Boyle; the penalties imposed by Cardinal O'Boyle varied from priest to priest, but included suspension from the active ministry in several cases. The priests involved took their case to the public and appealed to the authorities in Rome.

In April 1971, the Vatican's Congregation for the Clergy issued a document on "The Washington Case," which drastically minimized the nature of the dissent involved and "urgently" recommended that Cardinal O'Boyle lift the sanctions against those Washington priests who would agree to the "findings" of the Congregation's report. Those findings did not include either the obligation to repudiate previous dissent or the obligation to make an explicit affirmation of the moral truths taught by *Humanae Vitae*. O'Boyle removed the sanctions he had imposed on those among the original nineteen who still remained priests (a number had abandoned their ministry in the interim three years).

The Congregation for the Clergy was led at the time by an American, Cardinal John Wright; the Congregation's report and recommendations were the result of a lengthy negotiation between Cardinal Wright, Cardinal O'Boyle, and their intermediaries (two of whom subsequently became bishops). According to the recollections of some who were present, everyone involved understood that Pope Paul VI wanted the "Washington Case" settled without a public retraction from the dissidents, because the Pope feared that insisting on such a retraction would lead to schism—a formal split in the church of Washington, and perhaps beyond. The Pope, evidently, was willing for a time to tolerate dissent on an issue on which he had made a solemn, authoritative statement, hoping that the day would come when, in a calmer cultural and ecclesiastical atmosphere, the truth of that teaching could be appreciated. The mechanism agreed upon to buy time for that to happen was the "Truce of 1968."

History, including Church history, is full of "what if?" questions. What if *Humanae Vitae*'s teaching on natural family planning had been explained in the richly humanistic context that Pope John Paul II would bring to the discussion two decades later? Would the Church's teaching have gotten a fairer hearing? Would the dissent from it have been so strident and vocal? What if Cardinal O'Boyle had tried different means to maintain discipline among the priests of the Archdiocese of Washington? What if the press had not decided that the "man bites dog" character of "Catholic dissent" was a wonderful story line? What if a different mechanism for resolving this bitter conflict between a local bishop and his priests had been adopted? Catholics will be debating those questions for decades to come.

What seems clear now, however, is what the Church in the United States *learned* from the Washington Case and the Truce of 1968.

Theologians, priests, and nuns who publicly dissented from *Humanae Vitae*—who said that the Church's teaching about the morally appropriate way to regulate births was *false*—were encouraged by the Truce of 1968 to continue, even amplify, their dissent. There were going to be no serious penalties on fundamental breakdowns in ecclesiastical discipline. Theologians, priests, and religious men and women under vows of obedience could, in effect, throw a papal encyclical, a solemn act of the Church's teaching authority, back in the Pope's face—and do so with impunity. The culture of dissent, professional division, was born.

The bishops of the United States learned some things, too. Bishops who wanted to protect the authoritative teaching of the Church by using sanctions approved by canon law against dissenters learned that they'd better not do so if imposing those penalties involved major public controversy. Why? Because Rome wouldn't encourage such sanctions under those circumstances. At the same time, bishops inclined to encourage the culture of dissent (first on the birth control issue, later on others) learned that it was possible to do so, at first quietly, later publicly. Whatever its intent, the Truce of 1968 taught the Catholic bishops of the United States that the Vatican would not support them in maintaining discipline among priests and doctrinal integrity among theologians, even in order to safeguard what the Vatican believed to be basic moral truths, if the result were to be a public uproar. By this means, as well as by others, a generation of U.S. Catholic bishops came to think of themselves less as authoritative teachers than as moderators of an ongoing dialogue whose primary responsibility was to keep everyone in the conversation and in play. That, it seemed from the Truce of 1968, was what Rome wanted.

Catholic lay people also learned something from the Truce of 1968, even if they never heard of it. The tacit vindication of the culture of dissent during the *Humanae Vitae* controversy taught two generations of Catholics that virtually everything in the Church was questionable: doctrine, morals, the priesthood, the episcopate, the lot. More than a few Catholics decided that a Church prepared to tolerate overt rejection of a solemn act of papal teaching authority could not be that serious about what it was teaching on this or other matters. It was possible to pick and choose among those teachings that seemed most congenial, given one's circumstances and preferences. Thus "Cafeteria Catholicism" was another child of the *Humanae Vitae* controversy and the Truce of 1968.

Whatever the intentions of those who negotiated the Truce of 1968, the net result of this remarkable episode was to promote intellectual, moral, and disciplinary disorder in the Catholic Church in the United States. The lesson learned was that rejecting moral doctrines solemnly proclaimed by the Church's teaching authority was, essentially, penalty-free. Obedience to what the Church taught to be the truth, and obedience to legitimate ecclesiastical superiors, were now, somehow, optional. That disorder and indiscipline followed should not have been surprising.

DISSENT AMONG THEOLOGIANS

A second episode from this period, which involved a study of Catholic sexual ethics commissioned in the wake of *Humanae Vitae* by the country's most prestigious theological association, the Catholic Theological Society of America (CTSA), demonstrated how the culture of dissent had taken hold by the early 1970s and presaged its influence in U.S. Catholic theology for years to come. The study, published in 1977 as *Human Sexuality: New Directions in American Catholic Thought*, advocated a dramatic shift in the framework within which Catholic moral theologians thought about questions of sexual morality and proposed "helpful practical guidelines [for] beleaguered pastors, priests, counselors, and teachers." Both the study's theological conclusions and the guidelines flatly challenged longstanding Catholic teaching on virtually every issue of sexual morality, including contraception, masturbation, and homosexuality.

While *Human Sexuality* caused some controversy inside the leadership of the CTSA, the resolution of the controversy confirmed the influence of the culture of dissent. At the society's 1976 annual convention, members of the board of directors criticized the study's scholarship during their executive session. But board members feared that, if they rejected the study outright, their decision would be overturned on the floor of the convention by a resolution moved by the society's membership. The board agreed simply to "receive" the study rather than formally "accept" it, and the chairman of the committee that had prepared the study, Father Anthony Kosnick, agreed to a review by three moral theologians who would recommend revisions. In the event, the study remained essentially intact after the review. The study was eventually published independently by Paulist Press.

Human Sexuality also came under Roman scrutiny. In July 1979, the Vatican's Congregation for the Doctrine of the Faith issued an advisory on the book that deplored its "erroneous conclusions," identified numerous misreadings of the teaching of the Second Vatican Council in it, and argued that the study reduced the morality of sexual love to a matter of "personal sentiments, feelings, [and] customs . . . ." These theological errors led to practical guidelines that "either dissociate themselves from or directly contradict Catholic teaching" as taught by the Church's highest teaching authority.

How *Human Sexuality* did or did not measure up as an exercise in moral theology is not the point here (although it should be remembered that even scholars critical of some aspects of Catholic sexual ethics found the book a poor piece of theology). What was *learned* from the *Human Sexuality* episode was of more lasting consequence. Even if its leadership declined to accept and publish the study as its own, the Catholic Theological Society of America's internal agitations over *Human Sexuality* (which were widely known throughout the American theological community) sent several signals. The correlation of forces within the U.S. Catholic theological community was clarified. Dissent was, once again, affirmed as an appropriate response to authoritative teaching. Theologians who defended the Church's sexual ethic were put on notice that their dissent from dissent would be regarded as a betrayal of the theologians' guild. Younger scholars were told, in so many words, that a robust defense of the Church's sexual ethic would not help advance their careers, even if those younger scholars tried to work out new and more attractive ways to propose the Church's teaching on chastity and sexual love. Distance from that teaching, not an ability to present it in an intellectually satisfactory and pastorally compelling way, was the new criterion of professional acceptability in the CTSA.

The impact of this on priests was considerable. If the Church's best and brightest could not only dissent, but define dissent as an expression of Catholic fidelity, why shouldn't parish priests, who regularly faced the tensions between the Church's teaching on sexual ethics and the lives of their people, do the same? The influence of *Human Sexuality*, as an episode if not as an argument, turned out to be far greater than its authors could have imagined at the time of the book's writing.

THE IMPACT ON SEMINARIES

The Truce of 1968, the CTSA study, and the lessons learned from these episodes by theologians and working priests alike had a profound, and in some cases shattering, impact on the seminaries where diocesan and religious order priests are trained. As the culture of dissent reached critical mass in the American Catholic theological community, and as dissenting views on sexual morality and other issues were openly proposed as acceptably Catholic positions in seminary and novitiate classrooms, seminarians and religious order novices were faced with an almost schizophrenic situation. To be a witness to the fullness of Catholic faith now seemed antiquated, even bizarre. Orthodoxy, not heterodoxy, became suspect. Men who held firmly to the Church's authoritative teaching came to be seen as "rigid" or "ideological," and their own maturity and stability were questioned: Wasn't it a sign of psychological maladjustment that a man took the teaching authority of the Church so seriously? Didn't that itself indicate that he was repressing something? What was he afraid of?

At the same time, discipline within seminaries eroded dramatically. No sensible person doubts that changes were overdue in the instruction, spiritual formation, and regimentation often found in seminaries of the 1950s. By the late 1960s, however, the pendulum had swung entirely in the other direction. Daily Mass remained on the schedule, but failures of attendance were not deemed very serious. Few seminarians prayed the daily Liturgy of the Hours (Divine Office) they would be obliged to pray as deacons and priests. The practice of regular, private confession dried up (as it did throughout the entire Catholic Church). Devotional life— the rosary, the stations of the cross, Eucharistic adoration—

evaporated to the point where seminarians who still practiced these forms of piety were dismissed as "POD"—Pious and Overly Devotional—as one critical evaluation of a seminarian had it.

The data seem to suggest that these were also the years in which a higher percentage of candidates with homosexual orientations entered the seminary. Classic Catholic moral theology distinguished between homosexual acts (which are always sinful) and homosexual orientation (which is not deemed sinful in itself). Under the cultural pressures of the sexual revolution, however, and given the views of sexual morality promoted by dissident theologians, the act/orientation distinction got absolutized and the second half of the classic teaching on homosexual orientation—that the orientation itself is a disordered affection, a sign of spiritual disturbance—tended to be forgotten. As the rules for heterosexual encounters were increasingly relaxed in seminaries, it was but a short step before homosexual encounters, within and outside the seminary, were not regarded as serious offenses. In the 1970s and 1980s, some seminaries gained notoriety in the underground of Catholic chatter for their gay subcultures, which often included faculty members as well as students; Washington's venerable Theological College, once one of the most prestigious American seminaries, became widely known as "Theological Closet." Seminarians could now complete a four-, six-, or eight-year training course without ever having heard a series of instructions on the meaning of chastity, and without having had any serious formation in how to live celibate chastity after ordination.

Perhaps most critically, seminaries in the quarter-century after Vatican II became, in too many instances, places of intellectual deceit and self-deception. Because most bishops were unprepared to ordain men who overtly and publicly dissented from authoritative Church teaching, a double-standard slid into place. Candidates for the priesthood were expected to adhere publicly to the Church's teaching, but their theological training and spiritual formation had taught them that this teaching, especially on matters of sexual morality, was dubious if not utterly wrongheaded. Men thus learned, in the seminary, to pay lip service to teachings they did not believe and had no intention of promoting in their ministries. That this pattern of deception continued after these men were ordained priests should have surprised no one. Neither should the fact that intellectual self-deception helped prepare the ground for behavioral deceit and self-deception after ordination—especially in matters of sexual behavior.

The "Wounded Healer" Syndrome

Another image, drawn from a popular spiritual writer, helped promote the breakdown of discipline among priests in the United States in the decades immediately after Vatican II. Henri Nouwen was a Dutch priest and psychologist who taught for many years at the Yale Divinity School and lectured widely in Catholic institutions. A prolific and engaging writer, his books sold copiously. One of the earliest of those books, *The Wounded Healer*, proposed that priests should minister to others out of their own experiences of struggle in living the fullness of Catholic faith. The idea itself made sense—classic spiritual directors had done this for centuries—but given the American culture of the therapeutic into which Father Nouwen's proposal was launched, something rather different was learned from the image of the "wounded healer" than what had been taught by the classic spiritual masters.

Priests who came to think of themselves as "wounded healers"—especially priests who had been ill-formed intellectually and spiritually in the seminaries of the 1960s, 1970s, and early 1980s—were frequently tempted to give themselves a kind of pass on their "wounds." Sins like clerical sexual misconduct—once regarded as grave matters requiring repentance, serious penance, and a dramatically changed way of life—could now be considered "wounds" most appropriately addressed by a therapist, not a clear-minded and demanding spiritual director. That a priest is a "wounded healer" goes without saying, because priests, like other Christians, are sinners. When "wounded healer" becomes the center of priest's identity, however, something is seriously awry in his self-understanding, something that can lead to further intellectual, spiritual, and behavioral self-deception. The "wounded healer" who thinks of himself primarily in those terms gives himself endless tacit permission slips and ends up wounding others—sometimes in dreadful ways.

The clerical culture of American Catholicism arguably exacerbated this dimension of the crisis of discipline in the American priesthood. The extraordinary comradery and sense of fraternity found virtually everywhere among Catholic priests is one of the priesthood's most attractive characteristics. Priests are easily at home with each other, and that sense of fraternity often extends to real generosity of spirit: Priests support each other in numerous ways, talk the same language, have many of the same professional difficulties, share many of the same experiences, keep an eye out for each other. Yet, in a perfect example of how virtue can become vice, this priestly instinct to be supportive of other priests helped magnify the impact of the "wounded healer" syndrome. Priests who got accustomed to giving themselves passes on issues of sexual misconduct, on the grounds that they were, after all, "*wounded* healers," expected, and too often got, support in their self-deception (and their deception of others, including bishops) by fellow priests. Men who had grown accustomed to giving themselves tacit permission slips readily gave them to fellow priests. The clerical culture that had long promoted priestly fraternity also came to promote deception and defensiveness.

THE BEGINNINGS OF REFORM

The firestorm of controversy that broke out in the Catholic Church in the United States in the first half of 2002 masked the fact that at least some of the problems described here had begun to be addressed, and rather effectively, in the late 1980s and early 1990s.

Pope John Paul II's concerns about priestly formation in the U.S. led to a Vatican-mandated study of all U.S. seminaries in the 1980s. The study was ill-designed, to the point where some of the men responsible for the time of troubles in American seminaries, now bishops, were assigned as seminary visitators—hardly a prescription for reform. Yet the 1980s visitations of American seminaries did have some effect, alerting all but the most intransigent dissidents to the fact that the season of indiscipline was drawing to a close, and making clear the Roman view that a seminary simply could not be run without intellectual integrity, strong spiritual formation, and real discipline. And some seminaries began to change. That change was accelerated by the 1990 world Synod of Bishops on priestly formation and Pope John Paul II's 1992 apostolic exhortation completing that Synod, *Pastores Dabo Vobis* [I Shall Give You Shepherds]. By marrying a classic Catholic concept of seminary formation to contemporary concerns about human formation, *Pastores Dabo Vobis* gave a new generation of seminary reformers—including priests who had suffered during the silly season as seminarians or junior faculty members of seminaries—a real mandate for change, and one that could not be dismissed as impossibly old hat. When strong, effective rectors, committed to the high vision of priesthood promoted by John Paul II, took seminaries in hand, situations changed dramatically and, at least measured in institutional terms, rather quickly. One premier example of such change was at the U.S. seminary in Rome, the Pontifical North American College. In the mid-1980s, students there could be found dancing at parties—with each other. By the mid-1990s, the North American College was a model house of priestly formation, attracting large numbers of well-prepared seminarians for whom a vibrant orthodoxy was the solution to the Church's post–Vatican II difficulties, not the enemy. The difference was the leadership provided for a decade by two rectors thoroughly committed to implementing the teaching of *Pastores Dabo Vobis.*

The realities of clergy sexual abuse also led to diocesan personnel reforms that were largely ignored in the reporting on Catholic scandals in the first half of 2002. The 1985 trial and conviction of a Louisiana priest, Gilbert Gauthe, on multiple counts of sexual molestation sent sufficient shockwaves through the system that some bishops began implementing more stringent clergy personnel policies, and discussion was at least opened about a national set of such policies. That discussion was intensified by the 1991 case of another serial molester, the Rhode Island priest James Porter. At its November 1992 meeting, the National Conference of Catholic Bishops proposed creating a standard, nationwide policy with five criteria: swift response to accusations, prompt suspension of a priest when charges were buttressed by evidence, full cooperation with civil authorities, support for victims and victims' families, and frank public explanations of the Church's policies. In 1993, the Conference also established a committee on sexual abuse. But the Conference did not have the authority to compel individual dioceses to adopt its recommended criteria for handling cases of clerical sexual abuse, and while many dioceses did adopt those criteria, others did not. These changes in the handling of clerical sexual predators (which clearly sent signals to priests tempted to such behavior), coupled with the beginnings of reform in at least some seminaries, have had a positive effect: The proof is the relatively few cases of reported clerical sexual abuse from the 1990s.

But these modest advances were not enough. That they were not enough was evident from the gross mishandling throughout the 1990s of the cases of clerical sexual abuse in some dioceses, which was certainly not limited to Boston, Los Angeles, and Dallas. A deeper reform, based on a more thorough analysis of the roots of the crisis, is necessary. That, it must be hoped, is what the firestorm of early 2002 will provoke.

FAITHFUL DISSENT?

In the Truce of 1968, Roman and American officials tried to prevent an overt schism in the Catholic Church by acquiescing, at least tacitly, to the claim that "faithful dissent" was a real possibility for Catholics—including Catholics with official positions in the Church as pastors and teachers. What was tacitly conceded by the Truce of 1968 was explicitly asserted by the 1975 CTSA study, by two generations of theologians who taught America's future priests in America's seminaries, and, on occasion, by American bishops. The net result was precisely the opposite of the unity the Truce of 1968 had hoped to foster.

There was no overt schism in the Catholic Church in the United States, of the sort Pope Paul VI evidently feared. But there was a subtle, interior, invisible schism. It is one thing for a Catholic—layman or laywoman, seminarian, priest, nun, or bishop—to say of authoritative teaching, "I do not understand. Perhaps the teaching authority of the Church can make the matter clearer; perhaps we need to think about this truth in a more refined way." It is quite another thing for a Catholic—and especially a Catholic who teaches, administers the sacraments, and governs the Catholic people in the name of the Church—to say, "The highest teaching authority of the Catholic Church is teaching falsehoods and leading the Church into error." The Catholic who says, "I do not understand," concedes that, in the Catholic scheme of things, the Church's teaching authority is just that, an instrument of *authoritative* teaching. The Catholic who says, "The teaching authority is leading the Church into error" is declaring himself or herself out of full communion with the Church.

That is what too many seminarians and priests did in the quarter-century following the Second Vatican Council. They fell out of full communion with the Church, whether the issue at hand was contraception, abortion, homosexuality, or the possible ordination of women to the priesthood. If a priest is sincerely convinced that the Church is teaching falsely on these or other matters, or if he is simply lazy and absorbs the culture of dissent by osmosis, his conscience is deadened. And having allowed his conscience to become moribund on these questions, he is more likely to quiet, and perhaps finally kill, his conscience on matters relating to his own behavior, including his sexual behavior. When the incidence of such deadened consciences reaches critical mass in a diocese, a seminary, or a religious order, corruption—intellectual, spiritual, and administrative—sets in, as the culture of dissent seeks to bend the institution to its ends.

That is not all that happened, in the years after the Second Vatican Council, to create the current crisis of clerical sexual abuse and episcopal leadership in the Catholic Church in the United States. Clerical predators and malfeasant bishops are men who made choices for which they, not "the times," are responsible. The culture of dissent is a very large part of what happened, however. Historically knowledgeable and realistic people can understand that clerical sexual corruption has been and always will be a problem in the Church. But there is no explaining the breadth of the corruption that was brought to public attention in the first half of 2002, or the lack of effective leadership from some bishops in responding to it, without taking full account of the invisible schism that the culture of dissent created in the Catholic Church in the United States.

To be sure, that schism first took place privately, inside the minds and souls of many clergy and some bishops. What has now been made unmistakably clear are the schism's grave institutional effects.

Ideas have consequences. Dissent is a matter of ideas. Dissent, and institutional acquiescence to dissent, have had terrible consequences for the people of the Church and for the Church's public reputation. The crisis that the Truce of 1968 sought to avoid is at hand. No truce will fix it now.

CHAPTER FOUR

WHY BISHOPS
FAILED

T ENSIONS HAD BEEN GROWING for years between the Vatican and the leaders of the National Conference of Catholic Bishops in the United States when Pope John Paul II asked the archbishops of the United States to meet with leaders of the Roman Curia in March 1989 to air their differences and try to reach a common agreement on the role of the local bishop in the post–Vatican II Church. The differences, while they touched many specific issues, readily reduced to two perceptions of the situation. Some of the Americans felt that the authorities in Rome didn't fully appreciate the difficulties of a local church in a robustly democratic culture like that of the United States. Some Roman officials believed that the Americans had forgotten their distinctive role as authoritative teachers of the fullness of Catholic faith. John Paul II believed that an honest airing of these differences would make for a better working relationship between Rome and the Church in the United States in the future.

The basic issue—which was, as always in the Church, a theological issue—came into focus early in the special three-day meeting, on March 8, 1989. Setting the stage for the U.S. bishops was Archbishop John May of St. Louis, the bishops' conference president. "Authoritarianism," Archbishop May said, was deeply suspect in the United States. For the bishops of the United States to assert that "there is a Church teaching with authority binding and loosing for eternity" was a genuine "sign of contradiction" in modern American culture, especially as so many Americans, including Catholics, seemed to believe that "the divine right of bishops [is] as outmoded as the divine right of kings." That was the "atmosphere" in which the U.S. bishops worked, the archbishop concluded.

Cardinal Joseph Ratzinger, the Prefect of the Congregation for the Doctrine of the Faith and one of contemporary Catholicism's most distinguished theologians, responded to Archbishop May's paper. He was not persuaded by the archbishop's analysis. What Archbishop May suggested was a problem peculiar to the United States was in fact a problem in all modern societies, where the difference between authoritarian imposition and authoritative teaching was, at best, badly blurred. Why had that blurring happened? Because the contemporary world, rightly searching for freedom, had mistakenly identified freedom with willfulness—with doing things "my way." That mistake had led to a false impression, which had led in turn to an identity crisis for the bishops. The false impression was that *any* authoritative teaching was a partisan move in a power game. Fearing to be seen as partisans or authoritarians, too many bishops had taken to thinking of themselves as consecrated discussion-group moderators, whose primary task was to keep the conversation going and to make sure that all those involved were reasonably happy with the ongoing dialogue.

This was not only, or even primarily, bad management; it was bad theology. The act of faith was not a political act. Bishops couldn't call their people to be witnesses to the truth of Catholicism—the truths that the Church existed to proclaim to the world—unless they were convinced and effective witnesses themselves. Cardinal Ratzinger was unsparing on this point: "It is the hallmark of the truth to be worth suffering for. In the deepest sense of the word, the evangelist must also be a martyr. If he is unwilling to be so, he should not lay his hand to the plow."

Precisely because they were ordained to be evangelists, bishops had a responsibility to create room in the Church for serious "intellectual disputation," Ratzinger continued. Bishops also had "to be ready to learn and to accept correction." First and foremost, however, bishops had to remember that they were the guardians and teachers of an authoritative tradition—a liberating tradition that freed as well as bound those who accepted the risks and the adventure of Catholic faith.

In his opening address, Archbishop May had praised Pope John Paul II as an effective evangelist and witness, saying that "No one knows more about spreading the Gospel than you do, Holy Father." Still, the archbishop's evocation of "authoritarianism" and his strange identification of the bishops' consecrated mandate to be a teacher of Catholic truth with the absolutism of the divine right of kings suggested that Archbishop May, and those American bishops whose views he reflected, had missed something crucial about John Paul II. As priest, diocesan bishop, and Bishop of Rome, Karol Wojtyła had been an effective, magnetic evangelist because he preached a Gospel without apologies, with compassion but also without compromise. John Paul II had not become the most evangelically compelling pope in centuries by preaching Catholic Lite. He had become a magnet for young people and a moral reference point for the entire planet precisely because he spoke truth to power—political power, and the extraordinary power of the culture of "I did it my way." Moreover, he had backed up that truth-telling with the transparently honest witness of his own life.

The exchange between Archbishop May and Cardinal Ratzinger crystallized a set of issues that eventually produced the episcopal dimension of the Catholic crisis of 2002. Because of grave leadership failures by too many bishops, a serious problem of clergy sexual abuse that the Catholic Church could and should have take decisive action to correct was transformed into a crisis in which the Church's integrity was at risk. Episcopal misgovernance came in many forms: bishops who took a cavalier attitude toward sexual abuse; bishops who knowingly transferred sexual abusers from parish to parish and then denied having done so; bishops who misled other bishops about known sexual abusers; bishops who saw the crisis of clerical sexual abuse in primarily legal and financial terms; bishops who tried to deflect attention from their own culpability and buy media favor by raising questions about celibacy and Catholic sexual ethics; bishops who were all too ready to blame the media for their problems; bishops who drew insulting analogies between the common sexual failings of lay Catholics and priests sodomizing minors; bishops who, at least in their public role, showed a callousness and lack of pastoral concern for the victims of sexual abuse and their families; bishops who didn't listen to sound advice when they got it, or didn't know the difference between sound advise and stupid advice; bishops who let themselves be hamstrung by their bureaucracies; bishops who had failed to clean up their seminaries; bishops who had defaulted on their responsibility to be fathers to their priests; bishops who, when they were finally forced to address these scandals publicly, spoke the stilted language of law and the psychobabble of the therapeutic culture rather than the bracing, demanding language of the Gospel of sin, penance, and redemption.

Precisely because so many bishops became easy targets when

the crisis broke with full force in early 2002, it has to be said time and again that, when the scandalous behavior of abuser priests came to light in the past, some bishops took these matters in hand, dealt with them effectively, and built stronger local churches as a result. The diocese of Fall River, Massachusetts, which had been ripped apart in the early 1990s by revelations about one of the most accomplished sexual predators, James Porter, was on the road to recovery in 2002 because of the effective leadership of its bishop, Sean O'Malley, O.F.M.Cap. Lessons from the Fall River experience were not learned, however, a few miles up the road in Boston, the epicenter of the early phase of the crisis of 2002. Denver, which is arguably the most vital metropolitan archdiocese in the United States, had a series of sexual abuse scandals in the 1980s and 1990s; courageous leadership by two archbishops, J. Francis Stafford and Charles Chaput, O.F.M.Cap., turned what could have been a meltdown into a great opportunity for genuine reform, especially in the Denver seminary, which is now attracting vocations to the priesthood from all over the United States.

Other examples of the kind of leadership Catholics rightly expect from their bishops could be added. Yet even when those examples are noted the overall picture is deeply disturbing. Bishop after bishop in the United States failed to address the crisis of clerical identity, and the abuse and scandals that grew out of it, forcefully. Thus a serious problem was turned into a genuine crisis. While the crisis has many sources, it is also true that the bishops of the United States have led (and misled) the Church into the current crisis. If the way out of the crisis is to be a truly Catholic way, the bishops are going to have to be the ones who lead the Church from crisis to opportunity and from scandal to reform. What kind of men might do that, and how, is a topic for later. The question here is, *How could they possibly have done this?* Getting the answers to that question right will have a lot to do with whether the current crisis becomes the occasion for genuinely Catholic reform.

A Crisis of Identity

"Identity crisis" is a terribly overused phrase, but in this instance it cuts to the heart of the matter. Just as priests who truly believe that they are what the Catholic Church teaches they are—living icons of the eternal priesthood of Jesus Christ—do not behave as sexual predators behave, so bishops who truly believe themselves to be what the Church teaches they are—successors of the apostles, who make present in the Church the headship of Christ the Good Shepherd—do not behave the way too many U.S. bishops have behaved: as managers, not as shepherds who are also authoritative teachers. The core of the problem is captured by one of the unhappiest phrases in the entire crisis: the strange claim that priests are "independent contractors" rather than members of a local presbyterate joined by sacramental union to the local bishop for the service of the local church. Then-Bishop Edward Egan of Bridgeport, Connecticut, used the notion of priests as "independent contractors" in a deposition, in a legal gambit to protect his diocese from predatory liability lawyers. Whatever its merits or defects as a legal strategy, this misbegotten description of priests, bishops, their identity, and their relationship in the Church cuts to the heart of the crisis of clerical sexual abuse and episcopal misgovernance.

As always in Catholicism, the crucial questions here are doctrinal and theological. When a man receives episcopal ordination he is not, in the first instance, receiving a promotion. He is accepting, before Christ and the Church, a trust. He pledges himself to be the shepherd of a local church, the chief teacher and guardian of Catholic truth in his diocese, and a father to his priests (who place their hands in his at their ordination and pledge him their "obedience and respect"). That is why the Book of Gospels is laid on the bishop's neck during the rite of episcopal ordination. The Gospel is the yoke he has freely accepted in accepting the office of bishop.

No one should underestimate the gravity of the bishop's task, or the weight of the trust he assumes. He is responsible before God for the souls of those committed to his care, as well as his own soul. Indeed, his own salvation is intimately tied up with the salvation of his people. That is why bishops are given a ring at their ordination. The episcopal ring is not a medieval hangover suggesting a liege lord; the episcopal ring is a wedding ring, a sign of the bishop's marriage to his people, for better or worse, for richer or poorer, in sickness and in health, even to the risk of his life.

It is instructive that, as the crisis broke into public view in the first half of 2002, the widespread anger of U.S. Catholics was not directed primarily at their priests. It was directed at their bishops. That instinct was sound, and it cannot be attributed to a media campaign against bishops (however much some reporters, columnists, and editorial boards might indeed like to take bishops down a peg, or down entirely). The anger that Catholics felt toward their bishops confirmed that, even after decades of confusion about the nature and structures of authority in the Church, Catholics still expect strong, decisive leadership from men they have been taught to revere as shepherds. Catholics want to be faithful; they want bishops who will challenge them to be faithful, and who embody courageous discipleship in their own lives. For all the chatter about "democratizing" the Church from the culture of dissent, the anger of the Catholic people of the United States at their bishops is strong evidence for the claim that Catholics want, indeed demand, authoritative leadership from their bishops. That effective leadership is always leadership that earns trust, in part through broad consultation, goes (or should go) without saying. But the bottom of the bottom line remains the local bishop. That is the truth of Catholic faith that the great majority of Catholics in the United States have reaffirmed during the crisis of 2002.

"Headship" is a difficult concept for contemporary American culture to grasp, whether that be papal headship in the world Church, the bishop's headship in his diocese, or the pastor's headship in his parish. But when bishops fail to be responsible—and then fail to acknowledge their irresponsibility, or try to deflect blame onto "experts," or lawyers, or the media—Catholics understand, instinctively, that something is badly awry. That "something" is a default in headship, which is a more biblical word for "responsibility." When bishops are irresponsible, when bishops fail to be shepherds and heads of their priests and people, there are undoubtedly many factors at play, personal and institutional. The deepest root of the crisis of episcopal misgovernance, however, is theological—bishops have failed to live the truth of who and what they are. And they have failed to do that because they have not believed, with sufficient life-transforming power, the truth of what the Catholic Church teaches they are. Too many bishops in the United States have traded the rich evangelical, pastoral, and sacramental patrimony that is theirs for the mess of pottage that is contemporary management theory.

The Iron Cage of Bureaucracy

The crisis of episcopal identity, which has been thrust into the bright, unforgiving light of public scrutiny by the broader Catholic crisis of 2002, had been gestating throughout the post-Vatican II period. This itself neatly illustrates the principles that there are many ironies in the fire, and that no good deed goes unpunished, because Vatican II intended to reaffirm the ministry of the local bishop, who was not to be thought of by analogy to the local branch manager of a multinational corporation. Each local bishop, the Council taught, exercises true headship in his diocese; he is not simply the man who delivers and executes orders from headquarters in Rome. Thus one of the things that the current crisis tells us is that Vatican II's teaching on the episcopate has not permeated the Church as thoroughly as might have been hoped, even under the leadership of so dynamic a pope as John Paul II.

The theological crisis of episcopal identity was exacerbated by several other factors in contemporary U.S. Catholic life. Students of Catholic history will be sorting out the relative weight of these factors for decades to come. The crisis of clerical sexual abuse and episcopal misgovernance has, however, glaringly highlighted one of those factors—the intense bureaucratization of the Catholic Church in America at every level, from the local parish to the diocese to the national bishops' conference.

While there is probably no scientific survey on the question, three and a half decades of experience and anecdotal evidence suggest that the typical diocese today has at least twice, and often four or five times, the number of officials, workers, and bureaucrats as the typical diocese in, say, 1963. Some of this has to do with the expansion of the Catholic Church's social ministry and with a needed professionalization of some core Catholic activities, including education. It can also be reasonably assumed, however, that this vast expansion of ecclesiastical bureaucracy has a lot to do with the Catholic Church uncritically absorbing the general American tendency toward bureaucratization—and specifically the mainline Protestant denominations' extensive bureaucratization.

This bureaucratization has had numerous effects. It has required a tremendous increase in the financial resources directed toward Church administration (even though Catholic bureaucrats often work at wages far lower than they might command in society). It has made decision-making sluggish, as virtually every initiative from whatever source, including the bishop, has to be staffed-out, reviewed, run through committees, re-reviewed, and so forth. It has meant that priests and bishops spend an inordinate amount of their time in meetings; time being finite, that in turn has often meant time taken away from prayer, study, writing, teaching, preaching, and simply being present to the Church's people in homes, schools, nursing homes, and hospitals. This passion for meetings has also slowly and inevitably eroded the sense of headship among both priests and bishops. Structures intended to be consultative often act as if they were deliberative, and it is the courageous priest or bishop who is willing to insist, not as a matter of "authoritarianism" but as a matter of the God-given structure of the Church, that he must be the final decision-maker if the parish or diocese is to function as the Catholic Church and not as another denomination.

Bureaucratization has thus influenced what might be called the "denominationalization" of Catholicism in the United States. And this, too, has made for serious theological difficulties, for the Catholic Church is not, and cannot be, a "denomination" as the term is usually understood in America. A denomination is something with no fixed form, but rather a structure than can be changed at will by its membership; the Catholic Church has a form given to it by Christ, and that form involves certain truths (e.g., the sacraments) and certain structures (e.g., the office of bishop) that are not susceptible to change. That Christ-given "form" stands in judgment on the local embodiment of the Church; the local Church doesn't stand in judgment on it.

A denomination has other features that are, to put it gently, in tension with classic Catholic self-understandings. In a denomination, bureaucratic process is often more important than clear and binding doctrines. In a denomination, porous and shifting boundaries do not present serious problems because group-maintenance is the highest value and "being nonjudgmental" is crucial to keeping the group intact. In a denomination, effective moderation of the ongoing discussion about "who we are" is the most sought-after quality in a leader. None of these attributes of the American denomination has very much to do with the Catholic Church as it has understood itself for almost two millennia. Yet the Church today often displays each of these characteristics in one degree or another.

All of this has had a corrosive effect on the office of bishop in the United States, and specifically on the bishops' self-understanding. The current crisis has also brought to the surface another unhappy quality of bureaucracies—their difficulty in facing really serious problems. Bureaucracies everywhere are averse to confrontation. The grave problems of clergy sexual abuse, and the problem of the culture of dissent that helped make it possible, have made it painfully clear, however, that confrontation is what is sometimes needed. When the local bishop delegates key areas of responsibility to bureaucrats, even fellow clergy, he inevitably loses some part of his sacramentally conferred mandate to govern, and his leadership is inevitably weakened. This, among many other things, seems to have been what happened in Boston. The problem in Boston was not that Cardinal Bernard Law was "authoritarian"; one large part of the problem was that the cardinal delegated far too much of his responsibility to subordinates. A healthy dose of assertive, tough-minded episcopal leadership—"headship," to return to the proper biblical term—would have spared the Archdiocese of Boston being the epicenter of the early phase of the crisis of 2002.

CLERICALISMS OLD AND NEW

Old-fashioned clericalism has been a factor in creating the crisis of episcopal misgovernance in the Catholic Church in the United States; so has a newer form of clericalism, which is governance-by-bureaucrats. Bishops who mistakenly thought that their authority would be compromised by extensive cooperation with lay people with real expertise from outside the tightly knit world of the Church bureaucracy soon found themselves in waters deeper than they could manage. So did bishops who reposed excessive trust in the clerical subdivision of the Catholic bureaucracy. There are numerous Catholic lawyers and legal scholars of genuine distinction in the Archdiocese of Boston, as there are equally numerous and prominent New England Catholics who know how to make a public argument effectively. Yet the archdiocese had, by many accounts, seriously deficient legal counsel in sorting through its various scandals, and its communications strategy was below abysmal. The e-mails exchanged between Cardinal Roger Mahony of Los Angeles and several of his bureaucratic subordinates, which were leaked to the press and widely published, revealed the new clericalism at its most depressing—conversations conducted in a kind of strange code, intensely focused on "crisis management" and repairing failures of bureaucratic process, with little if any seeming acknowledgment that the problem of transferring known sexual abusers from parish to parish was a failure of headship that was causing grave religious and moral scandal.

The Catholic Church teaches that real and full episcopal authority is conferred on a man who is ordained a bishop and takes possession of his diocese in communion with the Bishop of Rome. Yet too many bishops in the United States seem to have forgotten that, while authority is conferred by ordination, leadership is earned by performance—and earned, and earned again, in a process of trust built up over time with colleagues and subordinates. Headship is a bishop's by the grace of Holy Orders. Effective leadership is something that he must display. And effective leadership can neither function nor be displayed if the bishop is hamstrung by clericalism in either its old-fashioned or new-bureaucratic forms.

THE TRIUMPHANT THERAPEUTIC

That Americans live in a culture saturated with psychological imagery (and psychobabble) has been clear since Philip Rieff's brilliant 1965 study, *The Triumph of the Therapeutic.* What the current crisis has demonstrated is how deeply episcopal leadership has been effected, and eroded, by the therapeutic mind set.

Six months into the crisis, more than a few bishops, including Boston's Cardinal Law, were conceding that they had placed far too much faith in the claims of psychologists and psychiatrists. Which was certainly true enough. Perhaps the most mind-boggling document to be released publicly during the early phase of the crisis of 2002 was the last clinical evaluation of pedophile John Geoghan from the St. Luke's Institute, a prominent therapeutic center in Silver Spring, Maryland, founded to deal with troubled clergy. Obtained by the *Boston Herald,* the Geoghan evaluation quickly made its way around the Internet. The conclusion of the evaluation's "spiritual assessment," by a priest who once headed St. Luke's, was at first dumbfounding, and then chilling: "Father [Canice] Connors notes that there are no particular recommendations concerning [Father Geoghan's] spiritual life since he is involved in spiritual direction and seems to have a good prayer life. The critical question for Father Geoghan seems to be whether he has ever integrated his psychological experience with his spiritual values."

A man has been raping children for decades and a Catholic therapeutic center has "no particular recommendations concerning his spiritual life," because the man's breviaries show signs of use and he talks with a spiritual director? Please. And then there is the matter of "integration." To the admittedly untrained eye, it seems at least as likely that John Geoghan's problem was not a lack of integration, but a spiritual life that he had managed, perversely, to integrate rather completely with his "psychological experience," his "spiritual values" providing no check against his pedophilia.

It was also striking that the 1995 "spiritual assessment" of John Geoghan by St. Luke's Institute did not probe the man's beliefs, even at the elementary level: Did Geoghan believe in God? Did he believe that God can make his will known to us? Did he accept the creeds of the Church and the Church's teaching on sexual ethics? Did he believe in sin? In punishment for sin? Did he understand the conditions necessary for making a sacramentally valid confession? Did he believe in his salvation, or fear for it? What was John Geoghan's theology of the priesthood? To, once again, the untrained eye, John Geoghan comes through in this evaluation as befuddled, what a teenager would call clueless. What is even more striking, however, is the seeming assumption by the priest-interviewer (a man frequently consulted by the U.S. bishops on sexual abuse cases) that these questions of belief have absolutely nothing to do with the "spiritual assessment" of a clerical sexual predator. Here was the triumph of the therapeutic at its most disturbing.

Why did the bishops of the United States repose such trust in psychology and psychiatry—among the most fluctuating of disciplines—in assessing cases of clerical sexual abuse? Why, in more than a few cases, did the bishops take counsel from therapists who were on the record as being in opposition to aspects of the Church's sexual ethic, particularly on questions of homosexuality? No serious person doubts that psychology and psychiatry can be of help in handling problems of clerical sexual abuse. The question is why so many bishops seemed to be willing to hand over such a high degree of analytic and decision-making authority in these cases to therapists. The cult of expertise in contemporary American society is undoubtedly seductive. But surely bishops who have taken to heart their vocation as spiritual shepherds ought to have exercised both more oversight and more caution in this area. Once again, the issue is headship, or, more accurately, defaults in headship.

THE TRAVAIL OF COMPASSION

The triumphant therapeutic reinforced a tendency among some U.S. bishops to divorce compassion—a Christian virtue—from theological seriousness in the exercise of their authority. The result was a forgetting of one important aspect of the Church's distinctive approach to the age-old problem of clerical sexual misconduct.

Ancient Catholic tradition, codified in the Church's canon law, has long held that certain grave sins by their nature disqualify a man from further public exercise of the priesthood. The issue is not retribution; the issue is iconography. A priest who sexually abuses children has grossly disfigured himself as a living re-presentation of the Christ who asked that the little children be brought to him [*Luke* 18.16]. A priest who sexually abuses post-pubescent minors in a habitual way is almost certainly guilty of the sin of seduction as well as the specific sin of sodomy or fornication. Don't habitual sins of this sort also render a man incapable of manifesting that spiritual fatherhood that is of the essence of the Catholic priesthood? These are fundamentally theological questions, not simply questions of "Church discipline." They have everything to do with what a priest *is*, which determines what a priest does— and what a priest must not do, at peril of his priesthood.

When a bishop has neglected his own fatherly responsibility to his priests, when he has been accustomed to treating clergy sexual abuse as a disciplinary matter only, and when the pressures of the therapeutic culture begin to weigh on him, a noble virtue, compassion, can be transformed into a vice— episcopal irresponsibility. The bishop fails to understand that some acts make a man unfit for any priestly ministry. And so the bishop recycles into his parishes (or to other dioceses) men who are both threats to their potential victims and irreparably disfigured icons.

Thus another disturbing aspect of the crisis of episcopal leadership brought to the surface in early 2002 is what can only be called the deficient theology of the priesthood implicit in some bishops' mishandling of the worst sins of clergy sexual misconduct.

ON NOT APPEARING "CONSERVATIVE"

For almost thirty years, the Catholic bishops of the United States have declined to accept the *New York Times'* editorial judgment that the Supreme Court's 1973 decision in *Roe v. Wade* settled the abortion issue. Instead, the bishops insisted that the abortion license was a matter of public justice, not of sexual morality, and that a private right to commit lethal violence (abortion) for personal ends (resolving the dilemma of unwanted pregnancy) was a profound threat to democracy as well as a grave crime against the victim (the unborn child).

The bishops did not simply make arguments on this front. They created and funded a pro-life secretariat in their national headquarters (led by smart, tough women), and established pro-life offices in virtually every diocese in the country. They launched crisis pregnancy centers and gave personal, medical, and financial help to women who sought alternatives to abortion; they also supported "Project Rachel," a spiritual renewal and counseling program for women suffering post-abortion traumatic stress. U.S. bishops were frequently found testifying in state legislatures and before Congress on the imperative of legal protection for the unborn and later, as the euthanasia debate heated up, for the terminally ill.

In all of this, the bishops served women in crisis and performed a great public service. By reminding America that its national story is a story of inclusion into the community of common protection and concern, the bishops' pro-life advocacy called the United States back to its noblest impulses. The Catholic Church is a major figure in pro-life movements throughout the world, but it can be safely said that no national hierarchy has invested so much in this cause, or advocated for the right-to-life so vigorously, as the bishops of the United States.

And yet that advocacy has had a curious effect within the minds of many bishops.

At the time of the Second World War, it's often said, no Catholic bishop in the United States was the son of parents who had gone to college. The parents of many of today's bishops may have earned their college degrees, but as a body, the episcopate still reflects the working class and lower middle class demographics of mid–twentieth century U.S. Catholicism and its deep links to the Democratic Party, especially in urban ethnic neighborhoods. Add to that the fact that several U.S. bishops were activists in the civil rights movement of the

1960s (perhaps most prominently, Bernard F. Law), and the fact that all of them are formally committed by the social doctrine of the Catholic Church to a special concern for the poor, and it is not difficult to understand why Catholic bishops in the United States, individually and collectively, have been extremely reluctant to be identified with conservative or neoconservative politics—which is where their pro-life advocacy would normally locate them. The overwhelming majority of U.S. Catholic bishops are, in a word, uncomfortable to the point of being upset when someone says that they're politically conservative. They don't, on the other hand, tend to mind being described as politically liberal, so long as it's liberalism with a pro-life difference.

This insistence that "we're not conservatives" has not played well, particularly in a media environment in which it is a settled matter than the abortion issue is *the* litmus test for sorting out left and right in American public life. The bishops' image problems (as they imagined them) with the press and with other American tastemakers were further exacerbated when Pope John Paul II declared in 1994, and in a definitive way, that the Catholic Church had no authority to ordain women to the priesthood. A Church that pro-abortion advocates had already labeled "anti-woman" could now be skewered as unrelievedly and hopelessly misogynist, thanks to the Pope's reaffirmation of classic Catholic teaching on this question. And this, too, was something that more than a few bishops found uncomfortable to live with.

Because of these multiple and conflicting dynamics, many U.S. bishops, feeling stuck in politically and culturally uncomfortable company on the pro-life and women's ordination issues, were eager to look "liberal" on as many other issues as possible. Yes, their own backgrounds and the Church's social doctrine—at least as conventionally interpreted by the bishops' national staff—inclined the bishops to more liberal politics on economic and foreign policy issues anyway. But the determination not-to-appear-"conservative" was at least as powerful a motivator among those bishops (and they were not few in number) who were not all that familiar with the evolution of Catholic social doctrine in recent decades.

This determination not-to-appear "conservative," which fit neatly with what bishops had absorbed from the therapeutic culture, seems to have created a fear of appearing "judgmental" and "homophobic" in dealing with cases of clergy sexual abuse. The bishops surely knew by the early 1990s that the overwhelming majority of cases of abuse had to do with the abuse of teenage boys and young men by homosexual clergy. Yet they were slow to act. Why? The determination to appear liberal on social issues other than abortion and euthanasia, and the fear of adding "homophobe" to "misogynist" in the standard American high-cultural vocabulary of put-downs of the Catholic Church, may well have blunted the bishops' ability to deal vigorously with the breakout of the scandal of clergy sexual abuse.

CLUBMEN

Anyone who has spent serious social time with Catholic bishops is likely to come away impressed. Many bishops are engaging, warm, informed, friendly, and sometimes very funny. Theirs is a special division of the previously mentioned fraternity of the Catholic priesthood. It can be a very attractive social environment.

It can also produce with bishops, as the dynamics of the fraternity did with priests, a defensiveness and a clubbish mentality that, over time, seem to have contributed to the erosion of many an individual bishop's sense of his headship and responsibility.

The impression of being an elite men's club is particularly marked, and regularly reinforced, at the meetings of the bishops' national conference. The bishops meet in the ballroom of a large hotel, not in a religious house or institution. They wear business suits, and if one erases from the mind's eye a sea of Roman collars, the meetings look like nothing so much as meetings of the senior officers of a very large corporation. The bishops' annual meeting, it must also be said, is conducted in precisely that way. Debate is governed by two traffic lights (red, yellow, green) which strictly warn a bishop that the time for his intervention is running out. "Debate," in fact, is the wrong word, for bishops' meetings tend to produce a lengthy string of individual interventions that may or may not have anything to do with what came immediately before, even if they're on the same general subject. There is, in other words, no real exchange on the floor of the bishops' conference. The occasional exception is in rare executive sessions of the conference as a whole; but then these executive sessions are closed to the press and to television, while the rest of the bishops' meetings remains open.

All of this reinforces an atmosphere redolent of a refined yet friendly club, an atmosphere that makes these men instinctively protective of each other and extremely reluctant to criticize one another's handling of problems—much less to call each other to account for what some may believe to be serious breaches of episcopal responsibility. The ideal bishop, at least according to club dynamics, is a man who gets along, doesn't make waves, doesn't assert himself theologically, and doesn't force decisions that others may be reluctant to face. The dynamics of the club also, if somewhat counter-intuitively, make the bishops even more chary than they ordinarily would be of their individual prerogatives: Local bishops have, traditionally, been extremely reluctant to concede even a fraction of their capacity to make local judgment calls to binding national policies. That, plus Roman nervousness about placing limits on the local bishop's legitimate prerogatives, is why the Catholic Church in the United States did not have national personnel policies for dealing with clerical sexual offenders when the crisis of 2002 broke.

The bishops tend to be clubmen in another crucial respect: Their instinct is often to talk with each other, and sometimes only with each other, about their most serious problems. The instinct is understandable in human terms. It is also an expression of Vatican II's teaching on collegiality—the bishops' shared responsibility for the governance of the Church, a responsibility they share with and under the bishop of Rome. It says a lot that is good about the genuine fraternity among bishops that they feel they can turn to each other when things go very sour. Yet in the case of clergy sexual abuse, the club instinct to take counsel only with other bishops ill-served the bishops and the Church. Knowledgeable laity, and priests who were not part of the new clerical culture of the Catholic bureaucracy, were rarely consulted—yet these were the very people who were in a better position to see what some bishops evidently could not see, or to demand that bishops see and deal with what some evidently refused to see and deal with. "Outside opinions"—in the sense of judgments from outside the bishops' club and the Church bureaucracy—were desperately needed. They were rarely sought.

The club failed its members. The members failed each other. Genuine collegiality, it turned out, meant something other than the pleasant, non-confrontational, and supportive atmospherics of a men's club.

A FAILURE OF IMAGINATION

There were undoubtedly many factors involved in the episcopal misgovernance that turned a serious problem of clerical sexual abuse into a full-blown Catholic crisis. Fear was surely one: fear of confronting malfeasant clergy, fear of publicity, fear of financial retribution from donors, fear of looking out-of-step with other bishops, fear of inadvertently doing something that would frustrate one's ambitions. In some cases, it is possible that fear of blackmail—either emotional blackmail or the real thing—was a factor in a bishop's seeming inability to come to grips with clergy sexual abuse, especially homosexual abuse. Misguided compassion was surely involved, as was a misplaced faith in the expertise of therapists. Many bishops seem to have had inadequate, and in some cases incompetent, legal counsel. Most bishops had had counsel from their communications staffs.

Yet these latter two factors, read correctly, cast the whole problem of episcopal malfeasance in the proper light. A bishop whose lawyers advise him not to meet with a victim of sexual abuse or with the victim's family because of possible legal implications needs different lawyers—lawyers who understand what a bishop is, and who have the legal wit and skill to make sure than when the bishop exercises genuine pastoral care and responsibility, he does not end up compromising his legal position or his diocese's. When the bishop does not understand that this is what he needs, it is the bishop who is primarily at fault. A bishop whose communications people tell him to make the most anodyne statements about sexual abuse for fear that any admission of responsibility would be turned instantaneously into a liability, legal or otherwise, needs new communications advice from people who understand that a bishop who forfeits his role as a teacher and pastor forfeits his capacity to govern at the same time. When the bishop does not understand that this is what he needs, it is the bishop on whom the responsibility of failure primarily falls.

In the final analysis, it really is a question of imagination, or self-understanding. And that, for bishops, is an irreducibly *theological* question. To repeat: A bishop who truly believes that he is what the Catholic Church teaches he is—a successor of the apostles who makes present in the Church today the living headship of Christ the Good Shepherd—does not behave like a corporate executive managing a crisis in which he has little personal involvement beyond the protection of his own position. He behaves like an apostle. He teaches the fullness of Catholic truth about sexual ethics, no matter how countercultural that may make him, and he does so in such a way that his priests and people are seized by the high adventure of orthodoxy and fidelity. He lifts up examples of fidelity and courage, so that others may be inspired by them. He condemns, forthrightly, what must be condemned. He embraces as a pastor the victims of abuse and he does what he can to help in their healing. As a father, he calls his priests to live the vows he and they have solemnly made before God and the Church. He shepherds the flock with a special shepherd's care for the weakest of the lambs.

The episcopal misgovernance that turned a serious problem into a crisis was caused by a loss of imagination and a loss of nerve. That loss of nerve had been evident in the previous three and a half decades of Catholic life in America: in bishops who approved inadequate catechetical materials, who tolerated liturgical abuses, who were frightened into passivity by theologians who taught falsely yet demanded to be considered authentically Catholic. Now, with the crisis of 2002, that loss of nerve has been publicly exposed. It is by no means the only part of the story of the Catholic bishops of the United States since Vatican II. But it is the part if the story that must be dealt with now, if a crisis is to become an opportunity for genuine reform.

For the bishops as for any Catholic, recovering one's nerve means recovering a passion for fidelity to the fullness of Catholic truth. Fidelity requires courage. And courage, for the bishops as for any Catholic in the modern world, means the courage to be countercultural.

CHAPTER FIVE

ROME AND
THE CRISIS

CONTRARY TO THE FAMILIAR stereotype, the Catholic Church is not structured like a pyramid, in which everything is decided at the apex and everyone down the pyramid—bishops, priests, nuns, laity—simply falls into line. The structure of authority in the Catholic Church is much more complex, and much more interesting, than that.

Take, for example, the question of papal authority. During the Second Vatican Council, Pope Paul VI suggested that the Council's basic text, the *Dogmatic Constitution on the Church*, include the statement that the Roman Pontiff "is accountable to the Lord alone." The Council's Theological Commission told Pope Paul politely but firmly that that simply wasn't the case.

Any pope, the commission pointed out, is also accountable to God's revelation, to the fundamental structure of the Church given it by Christ, to the seven sacraments, to the creeds, to the doctrinal definitions of earlier ecumenical councils, and to "other obligations too numerous to mention," as the commissioners delicately put it.

Among those "other obligations" is the pope's accountability to the moral law written into the world and into us. That is why, for example, the Catholic teaching on the morally appropriate means of family planning is not a matter of this or that pope's personal judgments. Popes are also accountable to the truth of things in general. A distinguished Catholic philosopher who thinks himself extremely orthodox once said, "If the Pope said '2+2=5,' I'd believe him." Another distinguished philosopher, just as committed to the papacy as his colleague, gave the correct and far more orthodox response: "If the Pope said '2+2=5,' I'd say publicly, 'Perhaps I have misunderstood His Holiness's meaning.' Privately, I would pray for his sanity." Popes, in other words, are not men who make things up as they go along. They are the servants, not the masters, of an authoritative tradition.

The relationship between the pope as the head of the college of bishops and the local bishops is also far more complex than is usually understood. As Bishop of Rome, the pope is both a member of the college of bishops and its head; indeed, the college cannot function as a college without its head. The college, on the other hand, with and under its head, has, according to Vatican II, real authority in and responsibility for the world Church, and so do individual local bishops. When a man becomes the bishop of Fargo, he assumes a responsibility for more than that slice of the Church that happens to live in eastern North Dakota; he assumes a responsibility, within the college of bishops, for the world Church.

There really is no secular analogy for the relationship of the pope to the local bishop and the college of bishops to the pope. The American governmental model—the pope as president, the bishops as a kind of Congress—doesn't work; neither does the British model, with the pope as prime minister and the bishops as parliament. The corporate model—the pope as chief executive officer of the international conglomerate Catholic Church, Inc., and the bishops as local branch managers—was rejected by the Second Vatican Council. Vatican II tried to explain the relationship of pope and bishops through the concept of "collegiality"—the bishops' corporate responsibility for the world Church—while at the same time teaching that that collegiality is always exercised with and under the leadership of the Bishop of Rome, the head of the college. It will likely take decades for the meaning of collegiality and its relationship to the pope's primacy to work itself out in the practical order.

So there is no pyramid. Many people, including many Catholics, still think there is, however. That is one reason why, as the crisis of clergy sexual abuse and episcopal negligence intensified during the first half of 2002, Catholics across the

United States were asking, "Why doesn't Rome do something about this?"

The question itself testified to the confidence that the great majority of U.S. Catholics have in Pope John Paul II. It also suggested that the same majority of Catholics were unpersuaded by years of anti-Roman agitations mounted by the culture of dissent, urging the Vatican to get off the back of the bishops' conference, to take the collegiality of bishops seriously, to stop micromanaging the Church in the U.S. Three months into the crisis, it was manifestly clear to many U.S. Catholics that their bishops were largely responsible for a serious problem becoming a crisis, that the bishops were incapable of coming to grips with the crisis on their own, and that they very much needed both the support and the prod of "Rome."

That prod came, eventually, in April 2002. It was, however, slow in coming. Why that was the case also raises interesting questions. The answers to those questions might not always be comfortable. But they, too, are essential to get right, if crisis is to lead to genuine Catholic reform.

OFF THE INFORMATION SUPERHIGHWAY

Popes govern the Catholic Church in collaboration with the Roman Curia, the collection of agencies or "dicasteries" (in Vatican argot) that are roughly analogous to cabinet departments in the U.S. government. Reading press accounts of its alleged influence in the world Church, one might get the impression that the Roman Curia is a vast octopus of a bureaucracy, with tentacles reaching beyond the Tiber to every nook and cranny of the globe. In fact, for an institution with more than 1 billion members, the Catholic Church has a remarkably lean central government: less than 1,800 permanent employees, from top to bottom. Of those 1,800, perhaps forty or fifty have real policy influence and decision-making authority—and the latter is always subject to the pope.

The top echelons of the Roman Curia are now thoroughly internationalized; the lower tiers of the bureaucracy tend to remain predominantly Italian. Everyone speaks Italian, which is the Vatican *lingua franca*. That, plus work schedules and work habits that mirror local custom, accounts for the dominantly Italianate cultural ambiance of the Vatican. Many of the senior officials of the Holy See are veterans of the papal diplomatic service, which adds another interesting element to the mix. For diplomats are famously conflict-averse and resolving certain situations in the post-Vatican II Church would seem to require sharpening, not blunting, conflicts—for example, with those who insist that there is a "spirit of Vatican II" that somehow transcends the Council's texts and, indeed, trumps the settled tradition of the Catholic Church. Veteran papal diplomats are prominent in the leadership of the Vatican's Secretariat of State, which Pope Paul VI turned into a super-bureaucracy through which virtually every other piece of

Church business passes on its way to the pope's office and personal quarters on the top of the Apostolic Palace (known in Rome simply as "The Apartment"). The Secretariat of State is also crucial in transmitting and executing the pope's decisions, for the Cardinal Secretary of State and his chief assistant for internal Church affairs, the *Sostituto*, are, theoretically, responsible for coordinating the work of the rest of the Curia in making sure that what the pope has decided in fact gets done, and in the way the pope wants it done. This requires strong leadership, which is not always characteristic of Vatican secretaries of state.

For all its internationalization, and what one might assume to be the broad flow of information that comes from that, the pope and the Roman Curia in fact depend on their colleagues "in the field" to give them a real sense of what is going on in a particular local Church—like, say, the Church in the United States. The two crucial points of contact in this respect are the local bishops and the papal nuncio (ambassador) in a country.

Every five years, every diocesan bishop in the world is required to come to Rome to pray at the tombs of Peter and Paul and to report to the pope, a process that also involves extensive meetings with Curial officials. For convenience, bishops from small countries come in national groups and bishops from large countries come in regional groups; in addition to a group Mass and a group meal with John Paul II, each individual bishop spends private time with the pontiff—at least fifteen minutes, often thirty minutes or more. No pope has ever spent as much time talking with bishops during these quinquennial visits as John Paul II; one senior Vatican official estimates that, in a normal year, John Paul devotes 40 percent of his public schedule to meeting with the world's bishops. But if the bishops are not frank about certain problems—if, for example, a significant number of U.S. bishops did not alert John Paul II to the real possibility that the incidence of clerical sexual abuse during the 1970s and 1980s could become a potential nightmare for the Church—the process of collaboration breaks down. The inability of the U.S. bishops to come to effective grips with this problem in their own conference was paralleled by the evident unwillingness of many American bishops to speak openly and candidly about this problem to John Paul and the Curia.

The papal nuncio also plays a crucial role in making sure that the pope and the Curia are well informed. When the nuncio knows the country in which he serves well, when he avails himself of many sources of information (and not just the information he gathers from the clerical fraternity), and when he reports what he has learned honestly to his superiors in Rome, the nuncio system works well. When the nuncio is not deeply familiar with the culture (including the press culture) of his host country, when he limits his information-gathering to ecclesiastical professionals, and when he fails to alert his superiors that a crisis is imminent, the system breaks down and the pope can get blind-sided by events.

The Vatican is also affected, and in ways that many Vatican officials have been slow to realize, by the new technological world of globally available and virtually real-time information, which creates expectations that could not have been imagined a generation ago. Americans are now used to living in circumstances in which major news events are instantaneously reported, information can easily be retrieved from a virtually limitless supply of online newspapers, online magazines, and Web sites, and interested parties are in frequent contact with each other about each breaking story and every groundbreaking commentary on it. American Catholics assume that their Church leaders in Rome are similarly plugged in.

They are not. As odd as it must seem, given the conventional wisdom that the Vatican is a wealthy and efficient bureaucracy, the Vatican is in fact way off on the roadside of the information superhighway. The Vatican officials who clearly understood that the U.S. Church was in crisis in the first quarter of 2002 were those who had spent significant time in the United States since January 2002, and those few officials who took the trouble to search the Internet regularly for information and commentary.

The Church in the United States expected that the Vatican was living through the American Catholic trauma of early 2002 in real-time, through adequate information from the Washington nunciature and through the Internet. The Vatican wasn't, because the Vatican is simply not part of the Internet culture and the information flow from Washington was inadequate. That created an expectations gap that widened and deepened during the first three months of the crisis to the point where faithful Catholics, ignorant of the information lag between the United States and the Vatican, were drawing the reluctant, indeed heartbreaking, conclusion that Rome simply didn't care.

OLD HABITS DIE HARD

What seemed to U.S. Catholics a sluggish Roman response to their trauma was also shaped by history and canon law. For, in another challenge to the conventional wisdom about the Church's "authoritarianism," canon law in fact bends over backward to protect priests from arbitrary and cranky (which is to say, genuinely "authoritarian") bishops. This has been a persistent problem over the centuries, and the canons have been written to ensure that every priest accused of an ecclesiastical crime has ample opportunity to defend his conduct and refute the charges against him. Canon law thus follows the venerable American legal principle that the accused is presumed innocent until guilt has been proven beyond a reasonable doubt (or, in canonical language, "to a moral certitude").

This solicitude for the reputation and ministry of priests is not simply the product of a history of episcopal bullying, however; it has profound theological roots. According to the

Church's doctrine, a validly ordained Catholic priest is a priest forever. His Christian identity is decisively changed. At his ordination, he is configured in an irreversible way to Christ the eternal high priest, whom he makes present in the world. Thus no ecclesiastical authority, including the pope, can strip a man of his priesthood in the sacramental sense of the word, for the priest is no mere hired hand or functionary; he is an *alter Christus*, "another Christ."

What the Church can do to a grossly malfeasant priest is, to use the canonical jargon, "dismiss him from the clerical state." That is, a man is forbidden from functioning, publicly or privately, as a priest, and has lost his legal claim on the Church for a living. He has been dismissed from the priesthood ("defrocked," in the inappropriate media image), although theologically speaking he remains a priest and could, say, administer the sacraments in an emergency. This drastic penalty is usually imposed only after a full ecclesiastical trial, which includes a right of appeal. Only the pope can dismiss a priest from the clerical state through a purely administrative process. John Paul II has used this power less than ten times in twenty-three years, but on two occasions pedophile priests were involved: Boston's John Geoghan, and Rudy Kos of Dallas. In 2001, the Vatican announced that new procedures had been established within the Congregation for the Doctrine of the Faith to expedite ecclesiastical trials in circumstances where rapid action was required against a clerical sexual abuser.

Lesser penalties against malfeasant priests involve restricting a priest's ministry—barring him from parish work, for example, or only allowing him to say Mass privately. In these cases, as with all penalties in canon law, the point is not so much retribution as a penalty sufficient to cause the sinner to repent, to amend his life, and to return to a state of grace—even if outside the "clerical state." Canon law shares American law's presumption of innocence, but it has a quite different understanding of the purpose of imposing penalties for crimes.

Over time, this legal regime has created a cast of mind in the Vatican that Americans find hard to understand, and that in fact makes it difficult for officials of the Holy See to come to grips with problems like the crisis of 2002 in the United States. That cast of mind, which it is no sin against charity to call "legalistic," was perfectly captured in a lecture in May 2002 by the dean of the canon law faculty at the Pontifical Gregorian University in Rome, Father Gianfranco Ghirlanda, S.J. Father Ghirlanda argued that bishops should not tell a parish that its newly assigned pastor had a history of sexual misconduct, if the bishop was convinced that the misconduct would not recur; that a bishop should not compel a priest to undergo psychological testing after a credible accusation of sexual misconduct has been lodged against him; and that the bishop had a grave responsibility to protect the "good name" of his priests by not publicly releasing accusations of misconduct, or even information about proven past misconduct, if it seemed that the offense was not habitual or likely to be repeated. On another tack, Father Ghirlanda said that neither a bishop nor a religious superior is "morally [or] juridically responsible for the acts committed by one of their clergy."

That Father Ghirlanda's view is widely shared in the Vatican may be inferred from the fact that he serves as an official consultor to four of the weightiest dicasteries in the Roman Curia (Bishops, Propagation of the Faith, Clergy, and Religious) and advises several other Vatican offices. Understanding that, in turn, may help Americans to understand why the Holy See refused the U.S. bishops' suggestion in 1993 that local bishops be given the authority to dismiss a priest through an administrative process rather than a full ecclesiastical trial in cases of grave scandal, like clergy sexual abuse.

To understand, though, is not necessarily the same as to agree with. If current canon law is admirable in its assumption of innocence and in its concern to protect priests from the arbitrary exercise of ecclesiastical power, current canon law as interpreted by Father Ghirlanda and those like him is manifestly inadequate to deal with the problem of clergy sexual abuse. Something has to change. Until it does, the Church's law will continue to shape the cast of mind of the Church's central bureaucracy in ways that make it difficult for Roman officials to come to grips with a crisis such as the United States experienced in 2002.

CULTURE WARS

The sluggish Vatican response to the U.S. crisis in the early months of 2002 was also due to important differences between American and European attitudes toward public scandal, including ecclesiastical scandal.

One way to parse that difference is to note that Americans remain capable of being shocked by the sexual shenanigans and misconduct of public personalities (including clergy), while European cynicism and world-weariness have generally muted similar reactions. That a recent president of France lived with a mistress for years was considered a non-story by the French press. The European media's bafflement over American outrage at President Clinton's affair with Monica Lewinsky was another example of a cultural divide as wide as the Atlantic. Europeans simply don't take these things as seriously as Americans.

That dimension of the difference may account for the fact that the European press paid little attention to the U.S. Catholic crisis even when it dominated the front pages of virtually every newspaper in the United States. An American coming to Europe in the first months of 2002 sometimes had the feeling of arriving on a different planet, not simply a different continent. What had become an obsessive topic of media attention and widespread public conversation simply didn't exist in Europe. Even those Europeans (and officials of the Roman Curia) who took the trouble to follow the U.S. crisis on the Internet necessarily missed a lot of the texture of the crisis, including the anger and dismay it was generating among faithful Catholics. One simply had to have been in the United States, to have experienced the crisis emotionally as well as intellectually, to sense that texture.

Europe's different legal environment also shaped and mis-shaped Vatican perceptions of the U.S. crisis. Liability law functions very differently in Europe, where awards of vast sums for "damages" of various sorts are not the norm, and where the phenomenon of lawyers making tens of millions, even billions, of dollars from malpractice or malfeasance suits is unknown. Europeans have many questions about the American legal system, but modern American liability law is something most Europeans find incomprehensible. That, in turn, led some in the Vatican, and in the Vatican nunciature in Washington, to the view that the whole crisis in the United States was manufactured by disturbed individuals and preda-tory lawyers who were primarily interested in money and media attention. On that analysis, this was something the Church could just ride out.

A PROBLEM OF COMMUNICATIONS

Cardinal Agostino Casaroli, Vatican Secretary of State from 1979–1990 and perhaps the most accomplished Curial bu-reaucrat of his generation, once said of the media, "We don't care what they print as long as we can do what we want to do."

It was a sentiment that would have fit well at the Congress of Vienna. Indeed, one could easily imagine one of Casaroli's predecessors as Vatican Secretary of State, Cardinal Ercole Consalvi, saying exactly the same thing to Talleyrand, Metternich, and Castlereagh while sipping champagne beneath the crystal chandeliers of the Schönbrunn palace in 1815.

Cardinal Casaroli was a very intelligent man, but in this instance he was gravely mistaken. What "they print" (and broadcast, and narrowcast, and stream across the Internet) has a great deal to do with what the Church can do (if not always quite so much as "they" think). It can create pressures to which the Church must respond. It can narrow the possibilities of the Church's action or, conversely, broaden them. Above all, what "they print" shapes the environment in which the Church must preach the Gospel and witness to moral truths in their impact on society. If that environment turns poisonous, the risks of failure in the Church's basic mission of truth-telling increase exponentially. To take the obvious example: Does anyone seriously propose that by Easter 2002 the Catholic Church in the United States was in as strong a position to shape the national debate over cloning, stem-cell research, and other enormous issues posed by the new biotechnologies as it had been in December 2001?

This generally dismissive attitude toward the press, which is pandemic in the Roman Curia, has been resisted by the head of the Vatican press office, Joaquín Navarro-Valls, a Spanish layman and former journalist. It has also been resisted by

Pope John Paul II who understands, far more than any of his predecessors and most of his senior Curial collaborators, the phenomenon that Navarro-Valls describes as the "dialectic with public opinion," which is shaped by the media. Still, neither the Pope nor Navarro has been able to change minds in the Vatican to the point where all the relevant parties agree that the Vatican needs a communications operation that understands the press's needs and perspective, and sees real possibilities for getting the Church's story out in a forthright approach to the media.

The classic Vatican attitude and its sometimes-grim effects were amply displayed on March 21, 2002, when Cardinal Dario Castrillón Hoyos, Prefect of the Congregation for the Clergy, presented John Paul II's annual Holy Thursday letter to all the world's priests at a Vatican press conference. Yes, the international press had vastly overblown expectations of this letter, and yes, too many reporters had been harping for weeks about the Pope's alleged "silence" on the issue of clerical sexual abuse. But did Cardinal Castrillón take the opportunity at his press conference to point out that John Paul II had in fact been talking volubly about the reform of the priesthood for more than twenty-three years? No. Did the cardinal point out that the Pope had convened an international Synod of Bishops to spend a month discussing seminary reform, and that the effectiveness of those reforms could be seen in the relatively few cases of clerical sexual abuse in the 1990s? No. Did the cardinal underscore that the Pope was not evading the issue of clerical sexual abuse by referring to the "mystery of evil" at work in the world, but describing the scandals with complete accuracy and in a way that resonated with the shattering experience of the victims of abuse? No. Did Cardinal Castrillón even suggest that the Pope was deeply grieved by the U.S. crisis, as everyone who knew him understood him to be? No. Rather, Cardinal Castrillón suggested that, what with the crisis in the Middle East and so forth, the Pope had a lot of other things to worry about. And in any event, the cardinal continued, it seemed that this issue was an obsession of the English-speaking reporters only, which could be saying something about their cultures.

An opportunity was thus turned into a fiasco. Even the most sympathetic reporters, prepared to write positively about the Pope's Holy Thursday letter and put the papal message in the proper religious and moral context, were infuriated by Cardinal Castrillón's dismissive attitude, his defensiveness, and his refusal to answer specific questions about the situation in the United States—for which the dicastery he heads had serious oversight responsibility. Some suggested that the cardinal's wooden performance had something to do with his alleged papal ambitions. It seemed far more likely that Cardinal Castrillón, an intelligent and personally courageous man who had once faced down drug barons in his native Colombia, was reflecting some of the worst aspects of the Curial culture in which he had worked for more than half a decade.

Cardinal Castrillón's suggestion that the whole American crisis was a creation of the mass media was not idiosyncratic. It was shared throughout significant parts of the Vatican. The inability to distinguish between American media hype (of which there was, to be sure, an abundance) and a genuine crisis (which was, in fact, the case in the United States) was another factor in the sluggishness of the Roman response in January, February, and March 2002. As a general rule, the Curia couldn't hold two things together in its corporate mind. Thus the corporate mind chose to believe what was most familiar: This was essentially a media circus whose time would pass.

An Oversold Product?

Finally, the dilatory Roman response to the American crisis of clergy sexual abuse and episcopal misgovernance was shaped in part by an excess of confidence in the Church in the United States, and in the U.S. bishops.

Contrary to frettings from the culture of dissent, the general view of the American Catholic situation in the Vatican was not deprecatory, but in fact quite positive, throughout the 1990s. The tremendous success of World Youth Day in Denver in 1993; the favorable response to the Pope's 1995 pilgrimage to Newark, New York, Brooklyn, and Baltimore; the continued vitality of U.S. Catholic parish life; and the emergence of a new generation of Catholic intellectuals bored by the classic agenda of dissent led many Roman officials, including the Pope, to an obvious conclusion: The Catholic Church in the United States was far more vibrant than in any other country in the developed world. That was, and is, true. But the picture was incomplete. What was missing from the picture was not inconsequential. And unless what was missing was discovered and addressed, it threatened the integrity of all the rest.

Similarly, the Pope and the Curia had a generally high impression of the U.S. hierarchy. True, there was no longer a great public figure like the late Cardinal John O'Connor of New York, and yes, there were still some bishops saying rather curious things from time to time, but from the Roman point of view the situation was quite different than in 1989, when the meeting involving the Pope, the Curia, and the American archbishops had been riven with long-festering tensions. The Church in the United States, the Pope and the Curia believed, had strong, effective leadership.

This, too, was a partial truth that masked a deeper problem. There were, and are, effective, charismatic bishops in the United States. There are bishops who, facing local scandals, have made a crisis into an opportunity for instilling a more integral Catholic faith in their dioceses. But there were also too many bishops who lacked the theological sophistication and communications skills to handle scandals like the scandal of clergy sexual abuse in anything other than conventional corporate crisis-management terms. There were also men who simply refused to see what was in front of them, for reasons of cowardice or fear. Their ineptitude, malfeasance, and misgovernance caused a crisis that everyone else, including the authorities of the Church in Rome, simply had to address, if the good work done over the past decade or more was to be saved and the achievements of the pontificate secured.

The turn toward the beginnings of that kind of understanding in Rome took place in a period of three weeks, in April 2002.

THE TURN

Arriving at the Vatican at Easter 2002, even a knowledgeable American sympathetic to Roman ways would have had to conclude that the senior officials of the Holy See were about three months behind the curve in assessing the U.S. crisis of clergy sexual abuse and episcopal misgovernance. Vatican officials seemed to be about in the same condition as most American Catholics in early January, when the Boston scandals were breaking into the headlines: confused, unsure just how much of this was real and how much was media hype, uncertain about sources of information, hesitant to believe that things were as bad as they might seem. Three weeks later, things in Rome had changed, if not dramatically then at least substantially.

The turn began on Tuesday, April 9. The day before, the Pope had had lunch with several American cardinals who were in Rome for the annual meeting of the Papal Foundation, a largely U.S.-funded agency that enables John Paul II to expand his charitable activities around the world: rebuilding seminaries in the former Soviet bloc, building AIDS clinics in Africa, and so forth. Conversation at lunch had naturally turned to the unfolding scandals in the United States, but the cardinals present—Anthony Bevilacqua of Philadelphia; William Keeler of Baltimore; and Theodore McCarrick of Washington, D.C.—did not seem to convey a sense of crisis. This was, they said, a time of "purification" from which the Church would emerge stronger. The tougher message was delivered at lunch on Tuesday by the president of the recently renamed U.S. Conference of Catholic Bishops, Bishop Wilton Gregory of Belleville, Illinois.

There were no preliminaries in this discussion. No sooner had the Pope said grace before meals than he turned to Bishop Gregory and asked, "What is the situation in the United States?" Gregory said that it was imperative that Rome understand that this was a crisis, in fact and not just in media perception. It was not going to be over anytime soon. More revelations of sexual abuse and episcopal mismanagement would be forthcoming. The Pope, who seemed determined that the U.S. bishops not face this alone, asked what he and the Holy See could do to help. Bishop Gregory, who was joined at lunch by the conference vice president, Bishop William Skylstad of Spokane, and the conference general secretary, Monsignor William Fay, replied that the bishops would try to adopt national personnel norms at their semi-annual meeting in June, and that the best thing the Holy See could do would be to give these proposed norms an expedited review when they were sent to Rome. The Americans were assured that that would happen.

The April 9 lunch did not discuss the roots of the crisis in the culture of dissent, nor did the heavy incidence of homo-sexual abuse get extended attention. Some might suggest that rather a lot of stress was being put on the capacity of revised personnel norms to resolve a crisis that involved malfeasant episcopal leadership and deep-rooted problems of fidelity and orthodoxy in certain sectors of the Church in the United States. But Bishop Gregory effectively communicated the es-sential, basic message: this was a crisis, not a mirage. In light of that the thought may well have occurred to the Pope and his closest collaborators that they had not been kept suffi-ciently abreast of the realities by the bishops and by the apos-tolic nunciature in Washington.

John Paul was determined to do more than make the creaky Roman machinery move faster after the U.S. bishops' June meeting in Dallas. Later that week, shortly after Bishop Gre-gory and his colleagues had completed their three-day round of meetings in Rome, the Pope accepted a proposal that an in-terdepartmental ("interdicasterial," to the Vatican) meeting be called in Rome for April 22–23, to involve Cardinal Ratzinger, Prefect of the Congregation for the Doctrine of the Faith, Cardinal Giovanni Battista Re, Prefect of the Congregation for Bishops, Cardinal Castrillón of the Congregation for Clergy, all the American cardinals, the leadership of the U.S. bishops' conference, and other Roman officials, including the Cardinal Secretary of State, Angelo Sodano. Responsibility for organizing the meeting was given to Cardinal Castrillón. The press immediately described this as the Pope "ordering the American cardinals to Rome," which if not strictly true (the cardinals were being summoned by Castrillón) at least helped communicate to worried American Catholics that the Pope was taking matters very seriously indeed.

The next step in the April drama came on Saturday, April 13, when Cardinal Bernard F. Law of Boston arrived in Rome secretly, five days after the Shanley case broke in the Boston press and created yet another furor. At lunch that day, Cardinal Law unsparingly laid out the situation as he understood it to the Pope, the papal secretaries, and Cardinal Re. That lunch, and meetings that Law had on Sunday and Monday with Cardinals Re, Ratzinger, and others, further drove home the message that a serious crisis was at hand. The same weekend, the Pope and his principal secretary, Bishop Stanisław Dziwisz, received a dossier of press materials on the crisis in the United States in its many dimensions; the dossier included commentary from prominent U.S. Catholics, known to be defenders of the Church and the pontificate, who were urging a clear-eyed view of the deep roots of the crisis and strong leadership in resolving it. Similar materials had not, it seemed, been forwarded to the papal apartment previously.

On Monday, April 15, news of the forthcoming April 22–23 meeting of U.S. cardinals in Rome broke and a media firestorm ensued. The Holy See press office was flooded with requests for credentials to cover the meeting, which many reporters and editors mistakenly assumed would essentially settle the crisis. These high expectations then crystallized around the phrase, "zero tolerance," which the press quickly decided would be the criteria by which it would judge the seriousness of the cardinals' response to the crisis.

Addressing the cardinals' meeting on the morning of April 22, John Paul II said that "the abuse which has caused this crisis is by every standard wrong and rightly considered a crime by society; it is also an appalling sin in the eyes of God." After expressing his "profound sense of solidarity and concern" to "the victims and their families," John Paul acknowledged that some bishops had in fact made decisions "which subsequent events showed to be wrong." However they refined the criteria by which they made such decisions in the future, the bishops and indeed everyone in the Church had to know that "there is no place in the priesthood and religious life for those who would harm the young." The Pope then turned to the problem of the culture of dissent: Catholics, and indeed everyone in society, ". . . must know that bishops and priests are totally committed to the fullness of Catholic truth on matters of sexual morality, a truth as essential to the renewal of the priesthood and the episcopate as it is to the renewal of marriage and family life."

It can be safely assumed that this would not have been said had there not been concern that some bishops and priests were not, in fact, "committed to the fullness of Catholic truth on matters of sexual morality," and that others were doing a very inadequate job of teaching and explaining that truth. On this linkage between the culture of dissent and the crisis of sexual abuse and episcopal misgovernance, as on the point about the necessity of reforming religious orders (where problems of sexual misconduct are quite probably worse than among the diocesan clergy), the Pope's address to the cardinals' meeting connected the dots in the crisis in a way that had not happened in the Vatican before. The call to a "holier priesthood, a holier episcopate, and a holier Church" was also noteworthy: This was a crisis of fidelity, John Paul was insisting, and the answer to a crisis of fidelity could only be a deeper, more radical fidelity.

By late Wednesday evening, April 23, the cardinals' meeting had produced a letter to the priests of the United States and a communiqué that summarized the discussions of the past forty-eight hours under six points: the U.S. bishops would propose a set of "national standards" for handling clerical sexual abuse cases, and would expect prompt action from the Vatican in reviewing them; the bishops' conference would devise and recommend a process for the quick dismissal from the clerical state of any "notorious" priest guilty of "the serial, predatory, sexual abuse of minors"; the bishops would also propose a new procedure for dealing with cases that were not "notorious" but in which the bishop had good reason to believe that the priest in question posed a threat to children and young people; a special Roman-authorized review, or "apostolic visitation," of U.S. seminaries should take place, with special reference to admission requirements "and the need for [seminaries] to teach Catholic moral doctrine in its integrity;" the bishops of the United States should pledge themselves to living the deeper holiness for which the Pope had called, and commit themselves to calling others to that holiness; a national day of "prayer and penance" should be mandated for the Church throughout the United States, to foster reconciliation and renewal.

By any reasonable standard it was an impressive communiqué, which made clear that classic pedophiles and habitual sexual abusers would be dismissed from the priesthood. The communiqué did not address the case of the one-time offender or the priest involved in a consensual sexual relationship with an adult who had repented of his sin and shown, over time, a truly reformed life. But in the nature of things, these were the hard cases and it could not be expected that there would be a one-size-fits-all solution to them that could be fitted into the format of a press communiqué. In short, the communiqué should have sent the unmistakable signal that things had changed and that strong leadership was determined on serious reform.

That did not happen, because the presentation of the

communiqué was an appalling demonstration of communications incompetence. The press conference was almost two
and a half hours late in starting, in part because of the
clumsy bilingual process by which the communiqué was
drafted. Only two of the American cardinals, McCarrick of
Washington and J. Francis Stafford, President of the Pontifical Council for the Laity, were present, along with Bishop
Gregory. When reporters naturally enough asked where the
other cardinals were, it was blandly explained that it was late
and they had other, unbreakable engagements. There was no
opening statement by Bishop Gregory— a violation of the
first principle of press conferences, which is that those
about to be grilled get their story out first, in a coherent
form, so that it's on the record and becomes a part of the
dynamics of the question-and-answer period. Someone had
decided that the fact that the communiqué had been quickly
duplicated and distributed to the reporters, fifteen minutes
before the press conference began, sufficed to replace an
opening statement. That it didn't was made unmistakably
clear, once the questioning got started. The result was that
no one watching the press conference on television had any
idea of what the cardinals had agreed to, even after forty-five
minutes of questions and answers.

Ill-chosen language in the communiqué itself caused further problems. The technical argot of canon law distin-
guishes between crimes of which no one is aware but the
perpetrator and the victim, and crimes that become publicly

known. The former are called "occult" (which has nothing to do with magic, but simply means "hidden") and the latter are called "notorious" (meaning, simply, "well known" or "publicly acknowledged"). Fastidious canonists among the drafters of the communiqué evidently insisted on using the term "notorious," seemingly unaware that, to the canonically uninitiate (which is to say, to virtually the entire audience that would read the communiqué), "notorious" would convey something very different from what specialists in canon law intend: It would suggest that the Church would take action against a sexual abuser only when his cover was blown by the victim, the media, or the prosecutors. Thus the clear determination of the cardinals' meeting to remove pedophiles and habitual sexual abusers from the active priesthood was lost, and yet another controversy broke out over why the Church would only take serious measures when "notoriety" was involved.

The cardinals' meeting in fact accomplished a considerable amount in a short period of time. That its impact was blunted (to be charitable) by an astonishingly inept presentation of its conclusions was very unfortunate indeed.

The Learning Curve

By April 25, 2002, five of the six points essential for understanding the crisis of the Catholic Church in the United States had at least been clarified in Rome. It was now broadly if not universally understood that the crisis was real: This was the Church's problem, not a problem artificially created by a hostile media. The Pope had made it clear that while the crisis had psychological, legal, and even political dimensions, it was, at root, a spiritual crisis—a crisis of fidelity. The demographics of clerical sexual abuse were better understood and its critical homosexual dimension was being openly discussed, if sometimes more tentatively than the facts should have suggested. The linkage between the impact of a thirty-five-year-old culture of dissent and the crisis in both its dimensions—clergy sexual abuse and episcopal misgovernance—had been identified, if not thoroughly explored. And it had become evident to virtually all concerned that resolving the crisis would require more assertive and courageous leadership from the U.S. bishops than had been the case in the past. What was not yet understood in Rome, it seemed, was that far more scandal was created by inept, and sometimes malfeasant, episcopal leadership than by the Church's frank admission that a bishop, even if not personally guilty of willful irresponsibility in handling cases of sexual abuse, could, by his bad judgment and bad decisions, lose his capacity to teach and govern. That issue would have to be addressed in the future, and indeed in the not-too-distant future.

Given the generally languid pace of the Vatican and the ingrained caution of Vatican officials determined not to do things in a panic, the learning curve in April 2002 was steep. That many important things about the crisis in the U.S.

Church had been clarified in three weeks was encouraging for those committed to the cause of genuinely Catholic reform.

That the pace of reform would have to be accelerated in the months and years ahead was also clear. So was the need for a comprehensive agenda of reform.

CHAPTER SIX

AGENDA FOR REFORM— SEMINARIES AND NOVITIATES

IN *PASTORES DABO VOBIS*, his 1992 apostolic exhortation on the priesthood and priestly formation, Pope John Paul II described seminaries and novitiates (the houses of formation conducted by religious orders) in richly biblical terms. Seminaries and novitiates, the Pope wrote, should be places where "those called by the Lord to serve as apostles [have] the possibility of reliving the experience of formation which our Lord provided for the Twelve." After calling the first apostles, Christ took them away for a period "to be with him" [*Mark*

3.14]. Thus the seminary, according to John Paul, "is called to be . . . a continuation in the Church of the apostolic community gathered around Jesus, listening to his word, proceeding toward the Easter experience, awaiting the gift of the Spirit for the mission."

It is a noble vision. It has, sometimes, been the reality of priestly formation. That this experience of going "away" with Christ to a special place in order to prepare for mission has not always been the experience of seminaries goes, or should go, without saying. That this is the kind of institution seminaries and novitiates must aspire to be, if the Church is to rediscover the courage to be Catholic, also goes without saying.

Many U.S. seminaries were in better shape by the mid-1990s than they had been in decades, thanks to effective leadership by those bishops and seminary rectors who undertook serious reforms according to the teaching of *Pastores Dabo Vobis*. For lack of such leadership, or because of the prevalence in them of a Catholic Lite vision of the priesthood, other seminaries remained troubled, and some of them are deeply troubled. The crisis of 2002 has made it abundantly clear that a deeper, more thorough reform of all seminaries and novitiates is necessary, if the Church is to have priests who believe and act according to the Church's understanding of their unique identity as icons of the eternal priesthood of Jesus Christ. That deeper reform involves virtually every facet of seminary life: vocation recruitment and screening; education for chastity and celibacy; human formation and growth in the spiritual life; theological education. It will also require close cooperation between local bishops and seminary rectors in the United States, and the relevant authorities in Rome.

APOSTOLIC VISITATIONS?

The U.S. cardinals' meeting in Rome on April 22–23, 2002, proposed that the Holy See undertake an "apostolic visitation" or Vatican-supervised study of all U.S. seminaries and novitiates. A similar visitation in the 1980s was less than completely successful, in part because the visitation team included men who had been responsible for the meltdown in some seminaries in the decades immediately following Vatican II. Such a situation cannot be permitted to happen again.

Seminary visitations will, presumably, be led by bishops. The bishops named as seminary visitators must be men who have already demonstrated an ability to reform seminaries, either as faculty members, rectors, or local bishops. These are the men who will know the right questions to ask, the sore points that must be probed, the patterns of reform that actually work. These are the men who will also know, from hard experience, the evasions to be expected—and how to deal with them. Fortunately, a good number of bishops with these qualifications are available, especially among the younger members of the American hierarchy. A seminary visitator does not have to be a prosecuting attorney. But unless a bishop understands from the outset that deep reform is needed, and unless his previous record indicates that he has the courage to confront what must be confronted, he should not be appointed to lead a visitation team.

Similar criteria should guide the selection of those who will make up seminary visitation teams. The seminary world is a close-knit one, including seminary faculty and administrators, diocesan vocation directors, and the staff of the national associations of vocation directors and seminary faculty. With rare exceptions it would be best to choose seminary visitation teams from outside the world of vocations "professionals," whose stake in maintaining something akin to the present status quo should be obvious to all. Effective, mature priests who have shown an aptitude for vocation recruitment and for guiding seminarians will make better team members for the visitation of a seminary than the members of the vocations guild. So will mature, experienced lay men and women with a demonstrated competence in professional education of various sorts, and an unambiguous commitment to the priesthood as the Catholic Church understands it.

If a prosecutorial approach is appropriate in these visitations, it would seem most warranted in dealing with the grave problems of some religious novitiates and houses of formation. When the "photo gallery" of novices on the Web site of the California Province of the Jesuits includes a kinky Mardi Gras picture of "Pretty Boy and Jabba the Slut" (finally removed from the Web site in early 2002 after a torrent of e-mailed protests to the provincial), the novitiate visitators may reasonably assume that something is seriously, even desperately, wrong, and that root-and-branch reform is imperative.

The visitation of novitiates and houses of formation for religious orders will be even more difficult than the visitation of seminaries. Many seminaries have already begun to reform themselves; the same cannot be said of many novitiates, as witness the fact that one novitiate felt compelled to post a notice in April 2002 cautioning the novices against imprudent cruising of gay bars. Historically, religious orders have enjoyed considerable independence and self-governance. But when the orders themselves demonstrate their incapacity to be self-correcting, the Vatican and the local bishops must summon the courage to step into the breach and demand serious reform. "Jabba the Slut" is, perhaps, an extreme case. The cast of mind that could tolerate that sort of behavior, produce such a photo, and consider it an appropriate form of vocation recruitment is not limited to the California province of the Society of Jesus, however. This cast of mind must be forthrightly challenged by seminary and novitiate visitators unafraid of being labeled "inquisitors," as they certainly will be by the culture of dissent.

RECRUITMENT AND SCREENING

While certain psychological screens are appropriate in assessing a man's potential candidacy for the seminary, what is far more important is an assessment of his faith. In one major

American archdiocese only a small percentage of the questions raised on a form sent by the vocation director to friends and colleagues asked to comment on a potential seminarian have to do with the man's faith and his ability to communicate the adventure of faith to others. The bulk of the questions, having to do with various questions of "personality," could be found on an evaluation form from the personnel department of any major corporation. Something is wrong here.

Surely the first questions to be asked of any potential seminarian involve his discipleship: How have you come to know Jesus Christ? What have you done in recent years to develop your personal relationship with Christ? Do you pray regularly? Attend Mass regularly? Meet Christ in confession regularly? What does your baptism mean to you? What does your confirmation mean to you? Do you believe that in the Holy Eucharist you are receiving the body and blood of Christ? How does that belief shape the rest of your life? What are your favorite Scripture passages? Why? Have you done any serious spiritual reading? Who are your favorite spiritual writers, and what have you learned from them? What was the finest sermon you ever heard?

The next questions to be explored with any potential candidate for the seminary involve a man's capacity for mission: Have you ever been responsible for someone else being baptized as a Christian? Have you ever been involved in someone's reception into full communion with the Catholic Church? Are you anyone's godparent or confirmation sponsor, and if so, how have you lived out that responsibility? Do you think of yourself as a witness for Christ, an evangelist? How have you lived out your baptismal call to bring Christ to others? Are you comfortable talking about your faith, especially with non-believers? Have you ever helped a fellow Catholic struggle with questions of faith, or with aspects of the Church's moral teaching?

Then there are questions to be explored about the priesthood itself: What do you think a priest is? How does the Catholic Church's understanding of the priesthood differ from concepts of the ministry in other Christian communities? What is the relationship between what a Catholic priest *is*, and what a Catholic priest *does*? What signs have led you to believe that God may be calling you to the priesthood? Do you think of celibacy as a price to be paid for the priesthood, or is celibacy something else for you? What do you imagine chaste celibate love to be? Have you lived such a life in recent years?

It should be obvious that the diocesan vocation director need not expect theologically sophisticated answers to these preliminary questions from a man exploring the possibility of entering the seminary. But these are the urgent questions to explore *before* psychological testing and screening begins. Unless a man is a reasonably mature Christian disciple, unless he has already demonstrated a love for Christ that manifests itself in a love for Christ's people, and unless he understands (if only in a preliminary way) that the priesthood is a call to a more complete emptying of himself so that Christ may work through him, there is little point in wondering how a candidate might score on the Myers-Briggs personality profile, the Minnesota Multiphasic Personality Inventory, or any of the other standard screens in the psychologist's kit-bag.

One young pastor, who attended seminaries before the reform of the 1990s took hold, reports that in six years of seminary formation he was never asked once what he believed about anything; his formators were concerned exclusively with his personality profile and asked questions drawn entirely from secular psychology. This tilt has been corrected in some vocation offices and seminaries, but the reform must be completed. From the beginning of the formation process, in recruitment and screening, theology must once again take priority over psychology in priestly formation.

The reform of vocation recruitment must also address one of the more bizarre phenomena in U.S. Catholic life today— the suspicion, in too many vocation offices, of young men who present themselves as self-consciously orthodox Catholics. To brand such potential candidates as "ideologues" is a grave mistake; to deem their deliberate orthodoxy a matter for psychological evaluation is even worse. Yet both of these things happen. Orthodoxy must, of course, be combined with pastoral sensitivity, intellectual openness, human maturity, and prudence. But young Catholic men, committed wholeheartedly (if sometimes clumsily) to the Church's teaching in its fullness, are not part of the problem of infidelity that was made painfully manifest in the first months of 2002. Their commitment to the beauty and liberating power of orthodoxy is part of the solution.

The diocesan vocation office must be a primary and ongoing concern of the local bishop, whose fatherly relationship to his potential future priests should begin years before he ordains them. Moreover, it is long past time to recognize that mature, spiritually compelling priests must be in charge of priestly recruitment and local vocation offices. In some cases, a bishop seems to have been eager to appease the local culture of dissent by naming a nun whose fidelity to the Church's teaching on the nature of the priesthood is not altogether secure to head a diocesan vocation office. This must end. Priests must be responsible for vocation offices in their recruitment of future seminarians.

EDUCATION FOR CHASTITY

In late April 2002, after four months of seemingly daily stories about scandal after sexual abuse scandal, a theologian at Rome's Pontifical Gregorian University, asked about contemporary trends in seminary formation, said that what concerned him was a "language of perfectionism that often sets [a priest] up for a fall." He then concluded on what he imagined to be a more positive note: "I think a lot has been done as far as teaching seminarians about boundary issues—that is, what is and isn't appropriate in relationships."

How will the Catholic Church know that the needed re-form of seminaries and novitiates has been taken in hand? Here are two plausible signs: when it is no longer deemed a matter of "setting priests up for a fall" to teach that vows must be kept, and when the "boundary" image has been per-manently retired.

Every Christian is called to a life of chastity, which the Church teaches is one of the "fruits of the Holy Spirit"—those perfections that the Holy Spirit works in us that are an-ticipations here and now of eternal life with God. Chastity is the integrity of love, the virtue that allows a person to love in a way appropriate to his or her vocation. For married couples, chastity is lived through faithful and fruitful sexual love. For the priest, chastity is lived through sexual continence.

Education for celibate chastity begins with deepening the discipleship of a candidate for the priesthood. Christ prom-ises that "if you continue in my word, you are truly my disci-ples, and you will know the truth, and the truth will make you free" [*John* 8.31–32]. That promise must be the foundation of all priestly formation, and particularly of formation in priestly chastity. If a program of priestly formation is first and fore-most a program of Christian discipleship, built on the firm conviction that the truths revealed in Christ liberate as well as bind, then candidates for the priesthood will grow into a ma-ture celibacy that is proof against both the corruptions of contemporary culture and the corruptions in the contempo-rary Church. A man who has learned to give himself away completely to Christ the Lord is a man whose heart, mind, and will have been trained to choose the good as a matter of habit—a man who can live chastely, as a celibate, even in a sex-saturated culture. Such a commitment is, obviously, a challenge. It is a challenge that can be met if candidates for the priesthood learn from the beginning of their formation that their lives as priests must be rooted in the mystery of Jesus Christ crucified and risen. That is not a misty piety; that is a bedrock theological truth.

Teaching about celibacy and formation for chastity in the seminary must take place within the context of a thorough and persuasive presentation of the Catholic sexual ethic. The Catholic sexual ethic is an affirmation of the gift of sexuality, insisting that sex reduced to another contact sport is dehumanized sex. The humanistic challenge embedded in the Catholic sexual ethic is best understood, not as a challenge to sexual self-control (a psychological category), but to sexual self-mastery, which is a moral category: the self-mastery that allows a couple to give themselves to each other in marital fidelity, the self-mastery that allows a priest to live his radical gift of self to Christ and the Church through sexual continence.

During the decades of confusion in American seminaries, the Catholic sexual ethic was neither persuasively taught nor, frankly, lived. The encyclical *Humanae Vitae* was rarely defended. Seminary professors of moral theology were prominent in the culture of dissent, communicating to their students that the Church's sexual ethic was, at best, one option in a supermarket of moral possibilities. Some of America's most prominent moral theologians, including seminary instructors, reacted to *Veritatis Splendor* [The Splendor of Truth], John Paul II's 1993 encyclical on the reform of moral theology, as if they were being asked to grade a term paper by a particularly dim-witted graduate student; the notion that the Church's authoritative teaching was the standard by which *their* work should be measured was utterly foreign to these theologians.

If a man has not been taught that the Church's sexual ethic is true and that the truths it contains are liberating—indeed if he has been taught as many seminarians were during the 1970s and 1980s that the Church's teaching on several hotly debated issues of sexual morality is false—he will almost certainly not teach those truths to others as a priest. And on the record that has been exposed during the first months of 2002, men malformed in this way will not live chaste celibate lives, either. The intellectual deceit and self-deception they learned in the seminary will often express itself in behavioral deceit and self-deception.

A candidate for the priesthood must have a firm conviction about the truth of the Church's sexual ethic and a demonstrated capacity to teach it persuasively to others before he is ordained. A candidate for the priesthood must have shown a capacity to live that ethic through a commitment to celibate chastity before he is ordained. These requisites are not only matters of assessing a man's willingness to be obedient, although that is not inconsequential. Because the

Catholic sexual ethic is an expression of the Church sacramental vision of all reality—the conviction that the extraordinary lies just on the far side of the ordinary, through which the extraordinary is revealed—a failure to grasp and live the Catholic sexual ethic suggests a deeper, more disabling failure: a failure to put on the Catholic imagination about a world "charged with the grandeur of God," as Gerard Manley Hopkins famously described it.

Within that Catholic sacramental imagination, in which the things of this world always point beyond themselves to the world of transcendent Truth and Love, celibacy can be seen for what it truly is: a radical gift of self that is a foretaste of life in the Kingdom of God. Life in the Kingdom is a perfect communion among persons and with God, although, Christ tells us, there "they neither marry nor are given in marriage" [*Mark* 12.23]. Celibacy lived "for the Kingdom" bears witness to this truth. Celibacy "for the Kingdom" is a living testimony that the grave or the crematorium is not the end of the story and that our bodies are destined for glorification in an eternity of perfect self-giving and receptivity. Living celibacy faithfully, the priest embodies the truth that Jesus Christ is the answer to all the yearnings of the human heart, and shows his people how all genuine loving points to the God who is Love all the way through. The seminarian formed in this concept of celibacy will understand that celibacy is far less a matter of not doing something (i.e., not getting married) than it is of doing something of grandeur: staking one's entire life on the promise of Christ, that "there is no man who has left house or wife or brothers or parents or children for the sake of the Kingdom of God, who will not receive manifold more in this time, and in the age to come eternal life" [*Luke* 18.29–30].

Forming chaste celibates in the reformed seminary of the future will necessarily involve a process of tough love. There will be no avoiding the hard facts of contemporary American life: that the celibate priest is inevitably a sign of contradiction in a culture which insists that sexual expression is a necessity. Celibate chastity is countercultural. The paradox is that chaste celibates demonstrate by their lives—by their affirmation that what they have given up for the Kingdom is *good*—that the Catholic Church in fact takes human sexuality far more seriously than the editors of *Penthouse* and *Redbook*. Thus the properly educated and formed celibate who lives his life chastely in service to others can be one of the instruments by which the sexual revolution's promise of liberation-for-love is redeemed from its own excesses.

HOMOSEXUALITY AND THE SEMINARY

The crisis of 2002 has launched another round in the argument about the place of homosexually oriented man in the priesthood, and specifically in seminaries. That argument is not an expression of homophobia, but the pre-crisis reluctance to face the scandal of homosexual clergy abusing teenage boys and young men was, in fact, a case of what some have called "homophobiaphobia." In any event, the argument is now engaged: Should diocesan vocations offices and seminaries screen for homosexual orientation and reject those men who declare their erotic desires to be homosexual or who are found by testing to manifest such desires unconsciously?

Addressing this question with both intelligence and charity means closing the gap that has opened up in Catholic thinking between "orientation" and "act." When a seminary formator or bishop says that the question is not whether a man has a homosexual orientation but whether he "acts out," the formator or bishop has made a serious theological mistake. According to settled Catholic teaching, authoritatively expressed in the *Catechism of the Catholic Church*, a homosexual orientation is a "disordered" affection, a spiritual dysfunction that has to be acknowledged as such and dealt with if a man is going to live chastely in the integrity of love. There can be no obfuscation on this point in seminary recruitment and priestly formation. However it may be regarded by psychology, theology does not and cannot think of a "homosexual orientation" as something inconsequential and spiritually "neutral." Moreover, vocation directors, seminary formators, and bishops must recognize the special challenges to chastity faced by a man with a homosexual orientation, given the aggressive homoeroticism of much of our culture and the patterns of promiscuity in the gay subculture.

Does that mean, as some bishops have recently suggested, that the Church should simply reject as candidates for the priesthood men with a homosexual orientation? No, it does not. The crucial distinction in accepting a man for priestly formation is between a man with a "homosexual orientation" and a man who declares himself to be "gay."

By the gay subculture's own declared self-understanding, a "gay" is a man who has made his homoerotic desires the center of his personality and identity; who manifest those desires to others; who defends those desires, and the acts to which they can lead, as morally worthy; and who himself acts sexually in homoerotic ways. Such a man has no business in a seminary. He is in dissent from the settled moral teaching of the Church, which means that he is not in full communion with the Church. He seems not to understand that an incapacity or refusal to imagine oneself as husband and father disables a man from giving himself as a chaste husband to his bride, the Church, and raises the gravest questions about his capacity for spiritual fatherhood in the priesthood. A self-consciously gay man in a seminary is also a disruption to others: a man who looks on his fellow seminarians as sex objects is not a man whose presence in a seminary is conducive to either genuine community or good order.

On the other hand, much confused air would be cleared if the Church would declare that a man of homosexual orientation who is qualified intellectually, who has not made his homoerotic desires the center of his personality and identity, who has been living a chaste life for a sustained period of time, who recognizes that his homosexual desires are disordered and has shown evidence of mastering them through spiritual disciplines, and who clearly manifests an understanding of the priest as a spiritual father is welcome as a candidate for the priesthood. Such a candidate would not, in a word, make a point of his homosexuality as a matter of pride or shame, either as a seminarian or later as a priest. Indeed, he would recognize that making such a point of it would impede his ministry. The formation of such a seminarian would have to take full cognizance of the pressures to act on their desires that contemporary culture puts on those of homosexual orientation, and it would equip a man theologically and spiritually to cope with the challenges he will regularly face.

As for the current seminary population, the worst possible response to the crisis of 2002 would be a tacit policy of "Don't ask, don't tell." There has to be asking, and there has to be telling—asking and telling done in ways that help a man discern whether he is someone of homosexual orientation, or whether he is "gay" and determined to remain so. If he is the former, an open discussion of his circumstance will only help him mature as a chaste celibate. If he is the latter, then he must be brought to the understanding that he is an inappropriate candidate for the priesthood, or he must be dismissed.

PUTTING PSYCHOLOGY IN ITS PLACE

The staff psychologist has been a staple member of seminary faculties for more than three decades, with the perhaps inevitable result that issues of sexual maturation have generally been remanded to this faculty member, or to his colleagues in the therapeutic community outside the seminary. This must change. While competent psychologists can certainly be helpful to a man's growth in human maturity, the assumption that such growth is identical with theological insight and spiritual maturity must be overturned.

Issues of sexual maturation and formation in celibate chastity are not primarily matters for the seminary psychologist, for in the context of preparation for the priesthood they are not primarily issues of psychology. Rather, they are primarily issues of theology, spiritual direction, and spiritual formation. Without a careful preparation in dogmatic, moral, and ascetical theology, seminarians will not understand the *why* of celibacy. As for spiritual direction and formation, it seems obvious that this kind of work is best done in seminaries by holy, mature priests who can teach others how to live chaste celibate lives. Nuns and lay faculty members may well be useful in other spheres of priestly formation; learning to live celibate chastity is best taught by chaste celibate men whose priesthood displays the qualities seminarians should emulate.

In any seminary, situations will arise where the faculty thinks it best to seek the professional help of psychologists or psychiatrists in dealing with a particular candidate's problems. The question of what kind of professional help is appropriate in these cases is an urgent one. Too many seminarians in recent decades have been referred to psychologists or psychiatrists who not only do not accept the Catholic Church's sexual ethic, but regard it as a prescription for psychological disturbance. This, too, must change.

Moral theology and sound psychology together suggest the appropriate criteria here. To be considered qualified to work with candidates for the priesthood, psychologists and psychiatrists should, obviously, be well-trained professionals certified by the relevant professional associations. They should also be men and women who agree with the Catholic Church on fundamental questions about the moral life and about celibacy. They should believe in free will, which means that they think that healthy, normal adults typically make free choices rather than "act out" under a variety of compulsions. They should agree with the Church that all sexual acts outside the bond of marriage are serious moral wrongs that harm everyone involved. They should acknowledge that normal adults can live celibate chastity in perfect continence. They should believe, with the Church, that people who make vows of celibacy should keep them (just as people who make marriage vows should keep them), and they should encourage their patients to do just that, rather than merely facilitating a patient's decisions.

Under legal and political pressures generated by the crisis of 2002, many bishops will be tempted to surrender even more of the Church's proper territory to the therapeutic culture. But surely after thirty-five years it is self-evidently clear that the answer to clerical indiscipline is not more therapy but more fidelity, more radical giving of self to Christ. The reform of seminaries is a matter of holiness, not of psycho-analysis or its sundry therapeutic offspring.

The Riches of Theology

The theological education of candidates for the priesthood must also be thoroughly reformed. Today's formation pro-grams (and especially those dealing with future diocesan priests) are not producing, in the main, priests who have a thorough grasp of the Catholic Church's rich theological heritage, and who see a lifelong immersion in that heritage as a vocational responsibility. Part of the reason why reflects the period of confusion in U.S. Catholic religious education in the two decades immediately following the Second Vati-can Council.

The typical theology course prior to priestly ordination lasts four years. For at least twenty years now, theology pro-fessors and seminary administrators have been complaining that seminarians beginning the first year of theology often come with a poor catechetical background. This should have been no surprise, given the silly season in U.S. Catholic cate-chetics and religious education that began in the 1960s and went virtually unchallenged for more than twenty years—a period that produced Catholic elementary and high school graduates who could not name the seven sacraments but who were quite prepared to argue that every miracle story in the gospels was a pious fiction. Few seminaries have sufficiently reformed their programs of intellectual formation to reflect this state of affairs.

Most seminary faculty are trained in graduate schools of theology and bring the critical approach to theology they acquired there to their seminary teaching. The result, unfortunately, is that too many seminarians are taught to deconstruct the Catholic tradition before they have even learned what the tradition is. Given what must be the assumption today—that incoming seminarians have had a poor intellectual formation in elementary and high school catechetics and (when they even took the subject) college theology—seminary faculties simply cannot continue to operate on the pattern typical of graduate schools of theology. The first thing that candidates for the priesthood must learn is the Church's doctrinal, moral, liturgical, and spiritual tradition. Only after they have learned the tradition can they fruitfully engage it critically. If a seminarian's theology program does not begin with learning the Catholic tradition, the result will be intellectual chaos and moral confusion—and yet another generation of boring sermons.

Perhaps the greatest failing of even reformed and well-run seminaries today is that their students do not graduate with the conviction that theology is their professional discipline, a body of thought with which they must keep abreast over the course of their priestly lives. Virtually every young doctor graduates from medical school thinking that a regular perusal of the *Journal of the American Medical Association*, the *New England Journal of Medicine*, and similar professional publications is simply part of his ongoing professional education. Very, very few newly ordained priests make the same assumption about keeping current with developments in theology, even through the secondary literature.

This attitude almost certainly has something to do with confusions in theological education, because of which seminarians not only failed to learn the Church's great tradition but became subtly suspicious of it. Seminarians formed in an intellectual climate in which it is assumed that modern thought is superior to all previous forms of thought will not think of Augustine, Aquinas, and Bonaventure as men they ought to continue to get to know during their ministry. Seminarians to whom it has been suggested, subtly or overtly, that "tradition" is a synonym for "obfuscation" will never get a sense of the Church's tradition as a living, developing thing, a conversation conducted within authoritative boundaries across centuries and cultures—and they will not be able to present it as such to their people when they are priests. Thus intellectually ill-formed priests contribute, overtly or inadvertently, to the notion that every issue in the Catholic Church is really an issue of power, when in fact the serious issues being contested in the Church are all issues of truth.

These confusions must be remedied if the future priests of the United States are to speak intelligently to one of the most well-educated Catholic populations in the Church's history. The remedies include seminaries securing faculty members who are unimpeachably orthodox, who understand the distinctive nature of theological education in a seminary, and who themselves lead lives of holiness as priests, religious, or lay Catholics. It is not a matter of intellectual repression but of common sense to insist that every member of a seminary's teaching and formation faculties accepts, and is prepared to defend, the most bitterly contested teachings of the Catholic Church today, including the Church's teaching on the impossibility of ordaining women to the priesthood and the Church's sexual ethic. Men and women who do not accept these teachings cannot adequately explain them to seminarians who are expected to accept them, and then to teach them as priests. To repeat, insisting on orthodoxy among seminary faculty should be understood less as a disciplinary issue than as a matter of Catholic intellectual integrity. Much of the culture of dissent has forgotten the Catholic sacramental imagination, whose recovery is so crucial to the reform of Catholic life across the board. It makes no sense whatsoever to nourish this forgetting in seminaries.

Theology, rightly understood, is not religious studies; it does not take a neutral stance toward the Catholic tradition. By the standards of the discipline, the religious and moral convictions of a professor of religious studies are of no greater consequence to his work than the religious and moral convictions of a chemist are to the study of inorganic compounds. Theology is different. Because theology is a disciplined intellectual effort to understand divine revelation, theology starts with revelation (as contained in Scripture and

Tradition) and is accountable to revelation. Thus the convictions of a theologian are intrinsic to his or her craft. This must be taken into account in hiring seminary faculty members. To assert this is not a matter of violating "academic freedom," nor is it a matter of banning speculative theological thought from seminaries; seminarians must understand that theology is a developing science. But all such speculation must take place within a determined conviction to "think with the Church," and within a clear understanding that the rule of faith is determined by the Church's pastors, not by the Church's theologians.

These same criteria should apply to those faculties of theology and theological "unions" or consortia where men in preparation for the diocesan priesthood or religious life sometimes study—for example, the Graduate Theological Union in Berkeley, California, or the Pontifical Gregorian University in Rome. While there have been some notable advances in the reform of those seminaries that house their own faculties of theology, the reform of these freestanding faculties and clusters of faculties has barely begun, and then only rather accidentally—because of a generational shift in which theologians who helped create the culture of dissent have moved into retirement. Even if seminaries and religious houses of formation are thoroughly reformed, seminarians and novices can still be intellectually malformed by attending faculties of theology where dissent from the magisterium is still considered a prime mark of intellectual respectability.

This suggests that a third form of apostolic visitations is needed, in addition to the visitations of seminaries and novitiates mentioned at the outset of this chapter: an apostolic visitation of all faculties of theology whose students include candidates for the priesthood, be they diocesan seminarians or religious novices.

In *Pastores Dabo Vobis*, John Paul II urged a more demanding intellectual formation for seminarians, principally in philosophy and theology. Priests who lack intellectual curiosity will not, he writes, be able to make "the Gospel credible to the legitimate demands of human reason." Thus priests must come to think of theology as their professional discipline, an indispensable tool in their ministry. By the same token, the Pope continues, theology is, at bottom, a means of nourishing one's personal relationship with Jesus Christ. This means that theology has to be done on one's knees, in prayer before the Blessed Sacrament, as well as at one's desk or in the seminary library. Theology must be taught and learned in the presence of the Lord, and must be nourished by an ongoing interior dialogue with the Lord. True theology—"speaking about God"—begins in prayer and ends in praise.

Thus theology, too, is a matter of growth in holiness. The theological education of candidates for the priesthood must reflect this. Otherwise, it will fail the Church and it will fail the priesthood. Reform, as always, means a return to roots. Theologians and the seminarians they train must rediscover the courage to be Catholic in living the adventure of orthodoxy.

CHAPTER SEVEN

AGENDA FOR REFORM— THE PRIESTHOOD

A S WAVE AFTER WAVE of clerical scandal broke over the Catholic Church in the United States in the early months of 2002, it was frequently said—if not always heard or reported—that there are tens of thousands of good and faithful priests in America—men who have kept the promises they solemnly swore on the day of their ordination and are spending out their lives in service to Christ and the Church. That is correct. To note this fact of Catholic life today is not, as some have suggested, an evasion; at least it need not be an evasion. The fact of priestly fidelity is every bit as much part of the story of the Catholic Church today as are the facts of clergy sexual abuse and episcopal irresponsibility.

The fidelity of so many priests is a great grace. It is also a tremendous resource for the reform of the priesthood that is imperative if the crisis of 2002 is to become an opportunity for genuinely Catholic reform. That reform cannot mean turning the Catholic priesthood into an imitation of the various types of ministry found in other Christian communities. The reform of the Catholic priesthood cannot mean making Catholic priests more like Anglican, Lutheran, Presbyterian, Methodist, Congregationalist, or Unitarian clergy. It can only mean a reform in which Catholic priests become more intensely, intentionally, and manifestly *Catholic*.

While clerical sexual misconduct has as many explanations as there are complex human personalities, the fundamental reality of clerical sexual abuse is infidelity. To repeat: a man who truly believes himself to be what the Catholic Church teaches that a priest is—a living icon of the eternal priesthood of Jesus Christ, the Son of God—does not behave as a sexual predator. He *cannot* behave that way. Yes, he sins. Yes, he is an earthen vessel holding a great supernatural treasure: he may give an uninspiring sermon, his choice of music for Sunday Mass may be deplorable, he may be inept in some of his counseling. But he does not use his office to seduce and sexually abuse minors. Nor does he engage in any other form of sexual misconduct.

The Catholic Church has long taught that what a priest *is* makes possible what he *does*—at the altar, in the confessional, in the pulpit, at the bedside of a dying parishioner. In an oddly ironic, even paradoxical, way, the truth of that teaching has been clarified by the scandal of clergy sexual abuse. If a man does *not* believe that what he *is*, by virtue of his ordination, makes the eternal priesthood of Christ present in the world, his desires may overwhelm his personality, and a life intended to be a radical gift of self can turn into a perverse assertion of self in which his priestly office becomes a tool of seduction.

Priests are made, not born. Although his discipleship must deepen during the course of his ministry, a man must be a thoroughly converted Christian disciple before he can be a priest. Discipleship is *the* prerequisite for priesthood. A Christian disciple is someone whose life is formed by the conviction that in looking on the cross of Christ one is looking at the central truth of human history—God's love for the world, which was so great that God gave his Son for its redemption. Convinced of that, a man considering the priesthood is committing himself to becoming another Christ, an *alter Christus*, another witness to the truth that God intends for humanity a destiny beyond our imagining: eternal life within the light and love of the Holy Trinity. That is why Pope John Paul II has insisted throughout his pontificate that the priesthood is about service, not power.

To put it another way, the priest must be convinced that the Church's story is not just the Church's story—it is the world's story, read in its true amplitude. A priest must believe that what Catholicism offers the world is not another brand-name product in a supermarket of "spiritualities," but the truth about itself, its origins, and its destiny—not a truth that's true "for Christians," or a truth that's true "for Catholics," but *the truth*. The Catholic priest who is a genuinely converted Christian fully understands that truth in this world emerges from many sources, including other Christian communities, other world religions, and the worlds of science and culture. The genuinely converted Catholic priest also understands that all those other truths tend toward the one Truth, who is the God and Father of Jesus Christ.

That is what he bears witness to in the world.

By his ordination and his vow of celibacy, the Catholic priest is set apart from the world for the world's sake. In a culture like ours, his life is a sign of contradiction to much of what the world imagines to be true. The priest is not a contrarian, however. His being different is not an end in itself, an indulgence in idiosyncracy. The priest is a sign of contradiction so that the world can learn the truth about itself—so that the world can be converted. The radical openness to serve others that should be manifest in a happy, holy priest's life is a living lesson to the world that self-giving, not self-assertion, is the royal road to human flourishing. The priest's obedience to the truths of faith, and the liberating power that unleashes in him to be a man for others, reminds the world that truth binds and frees at the same time. Lived in integrity, the priest's celibacy is a powerful witness to the truth that there are things worth dying for—including dying-to-self for. The priest's renunciation of the good of marital communion and the good of physical paternity is a reminder that those two things are, in fact, *good*, and should make possible in him a genuine and generous spiritual paternity.

By teaching the truths of Catholic faith, by sanctifying his people through the sacraments, and by governing justly that portion of God's people entrusted to his pastoral authority, the Catholic priest enables men and women to become saints—to become the kind of people who can live with God forever. That, the Catholic Church teaches, is what God intended for all humanity "from the beginning." That is why the Son of God entered history to redeem the world. That is why the Holy Spirit sanctifies the Church and, through the Church, the world. All of this is intended to prepare men and women for eternal life in perfect communion with each other and with God. All of this is intended to make saints—better, to cooperate with God in God's making of saints.

That is what a Catholic priest is for. And that is why a Catholic priest must understand himself to be what he is—a living icon of the eternal priesthood of Christ—and order his life, in all its facets, according to that awesome truth.

A Continuing Education

"Continuing priestly education" has been something of a buzzword in U.S. Catholic circles for a quarter of a century or more. The phrase reflects the conviction that a man's education in and for the priesthood does not end on the day of his ordination, but must continue throughout his priestly service. Like the Second Vatican Council itself (and to borrow two bits of Council-jargon), continuing priestly education is a matter of both *aggiornamento* (updating) and *ressourcement* (a return to the ancient sources of Christian wisdom). Unhappily, a lot of continuing priestly education over the past several decades has stressed the former, sometimes in bizarre forms, to the forgetting of the latter.

The reform of the priesthood must include continuing priestly education programs that ignore the Eneagram and other gimmicks of pop psychology and "spirituality" in order to focus intensely on deepening a man's theological understanding of himself and his priesthood—its New Testament origins, its historical development, and the best contemporary analyses of this unique vocation. Even those continuing education programs that don't fall into the trap of psychobabble tend to stress craft over thick theological substance. This must be reversed. Effective liturgical, administrative, preaching, and pastoral techniques can be readily learned from other priests. Serious continuing education for priests—from week-long seminars to six-month sabbaticals—must focus in the future on theology.

This is especially important for those priests whose theological education took place during the decades of confusion in seminaries that ran from the mid-1960s to the later 1980s (and, in some instances, beyond). It is the rare priest from that era who is well-grounded in classic Catholic theology. That, and continuing education programs that have failed to fill in the blanks, helps explain one of the odder phenomena of contemporary Catholic life in the United States—lay people using the *Catechism of the Catholic Church* to challenge the doctrinal curiosities they sometimes hear from the pulpit. The generation of priests ordained between the early 1970s and late 1980s includes many fine pastors who have been cheated of their theological birthright as priests. The reform of the Catholic priesthood in the twenty-first century requires restoring that birthright to them, through theologically centered continuing education.

The local bishop must take the lead in providing for the continuing theological and pastoral education of his priests, ensuring orthodoxy in what is taught and lending his support (and, ideally) his presence to programs of continuing priestly education, so that his priests understand that he, too, is part of a presbyterate of learners who seek to deepen their relationship to Jesus Christ through a deeper study of the Church's tradition. The bishop's role in the continuing formation of priests goes beyond providing for formal programs, however.

While the priest must himself be the chief agent of his ongoing education and formation, an honest, open, intimate relationship with his bishop is also a crucial part of any priest's lifelong work of remaining faithful to his vocation and his vows. This will require, in some cases, new understandings on the part of both priests and bishops. One of the local bishop's most urgent responsibilities is to make every possible effort to assist his priests in living every aspect of their lives according to the Gospel. Moreover, this kind of spiritual accountability has to be understood by both priests and bishops as an integral part of their relationship, not as some kind of illegitimate or intrusive interference from an "employer" in a priest's "private life."

Like any good father, the bishop must ask his spiritual sons specific, concrete, detailed questions about the manner in which they are living their priestly vocations: How often do you pray? Do you have a spiritual director whom you see regularly? Are you sleeping alone? Is Internet pornography a troublesome temptation? Is your recreation appropriate for a priest? Are your friendships, with both priests and laity, morally blameworthy? Do you have problems with alcohol? Is your celibacy fulfilling or burdensome, and are you living it faithfully and peacefully?

If those questions are asked in the context of genuine spiritual fatherhood—if the bishop has shown himself to his priests as a pastor and father, not simply an ecclesiastical executive—a priest will understand that his bishop is seeking the good of the Church in probing his life so carefully, and he will understand that answering frankly is a benefit to his diocese, his fellow priests, and his own priesthood.

DEEPENING FRATERNITY

The brotherhood of the Catholic priesthood is both a good in itself and an opportunity for reformed continuing education. A number of different types of "priest support groups" have flourished in the United States since Vatican II, primarily focused on problem-sharing and enriching priests' spiritual lives. Were serious theological study added to these programs, they would constitute an even more powerful instrument of deepening priestly identity and priestly fraternity.

By the same token, when the priests of a local diocese are bitterly divided over questions of doctrine, morality, and liturgical practice, they become estranged from the very men to whom they should be closest. And, in today's culture, a single man, often living alone, estranged from those who ought to be his friends and supporters, is a man vulnerable to temptations to sexual misconduct of various sorts.

Here, again, the local bishop's role is crucial. If the bishop imagines that his primary function is to keep the presbyterate reasonably placid by keeping everyone in the conversation, he will not be in a position to close the rifts that exist because of some priests' unorthodox views, strange liturgical behavior, or inappropriate conduct. The unity worth nurturing and deepening among the priests of a diocese is unity in truth: in preaching and teaching the fullness of Catholic faith, in the observance of liturgical norms, in upright personal behavior. The best thing some bishops could do for the fraternity of their priests is to challenge forthrightly those priests whose thinking and lifestyles suggest that their full communion with the Church is defective. That challenge is the precondition to their returning, with the help of their priestly brothers, to a more integral living of their unique vocation.

WELCOMING THE NEWLY ORDAINED

The experience of priestly fraternity is particularly important for young priests. One of the most serious problems Catholic priests in the United States face today is loneliness, as more and more parishes become "one-priest" parishes. Loneliness, in turn, is a breeding ground for temptation. The local bishop and his priests' council must make a concerted effort to see that priests are in contact with each other regularly, and that young priests in particular are embraced in the fraternity of the priesthood and supported by their fellow priests in the crucial, early years of their ministry.

It is unconscionable for a bishop to assign a recently or-dained priest to live by himself in a rectory, as sometimes hap-pens. Indeed, insofar as is humanly possible, no priest should be assigned to a one-priest parish until he has successfully completed five years of priestly ministry, and preferably ten. If making provision for that means lengthening some priests' terms of service beyond the now-typical retirement age of seventy, then that, too, must be done. Moreover, newly or-dained priests must spend the first years of their priesthood in parishes, not in chancery offices or as bishop's secretaries. If a young man really wants to live the early years of his priest-hood as a bureaucrat or an ordained chauffeur, that is almost certainly a sign that something is defective in his vocational discernment or formation. The bishop has a special paternal responsibility to his new priests, and exercising that responsibility includes ensuring that the newly ordained receive ample opportunities to be what they now are, and to do the things that only they can do—which means parish and school chaplaincy work, not a quick segué onto the career fast track of the local Catholic bureaucracy.

Beyond that the local bishop should revive an ancient practice by meeting regularly with his new priests and conducting the first phase of their continuing priestly education himself. What was good enough for Augustine when he was bishop of Hippo in the fifth century should commend itself to bishops of the twenty-first century. While the bishop has an obligation to be present regularly to all his priests, bishops who make themselves responsible in a direct, personal way for the continuing education of their newly ordained priests are bishops who will be building strong, vital presbyterates for the future.

ASCETICISM AND LIFESTYLE

The reform of the Catholic priesthood in the United States is also going to require a close, critical look at the way priests typically live today.

There is no one-size-fits-all model of priestly asceticism that is appropriate to the enormous variety of circumstances in which priests live out their vocations in contemporary

America. What can be said is that asceticism—the deliberate choice of a way of life that requires disciplined self-sacrifice across the board—is essential in each of those circumstances. Priestly asceticism cannot be thought of as a matter of sexual continence alone. Indeed, a priest is far less likely to live his vows of celibate chastity faithfully unless he is living ascetically, and by personal choice, in other aspects of his life: dress, possessions, approach to alcohol, choice of companions and recreation.

Asceticism for the priest begins where it does for every Christian—with prayer. During the early months of the crisis of 2002, a distinguished priest-theologian, Father Matthew Lamb, wrote the following for the *Boston College Chronicle*: "I wager that NONE of the priests who perpetrated these sins and crimes fulfilled the following five requirements for a good priestly life in Christ: (1) reverently celebrate daily Mass; (2) pray the Divine Office daily; (3) spend an hour each day in prayerful communion with the Triune God; (4) nourish their minds and hearts with daily readings from Holy Scripture and the writings of the great saints and scholars of Catholic wisdom; (5) daily examination of conscience to deepen their awareness of being a sinner forgiven by God's grace, along with regular sacramental confession and spiritual direction." Judging from press reports of the lifestyles of some clerical sexual predators, no scientific survey is required to conclude that Father Lamb was making a very safe bet here. He then drew the appropriate conclusion: "No amount of so-called structural reforms will go to the roots of this scandalous crisis if they ignore the fundamental importance of these five daily elements in an authentic priestly life and practice."

A priest cannot be a man for others if he lives as others often live. His dress, his comportment (privately as well as publicly), and above all his prayer must reflect a daily determination to renounce many goods for the sake of the Kingdom. This does not mean that parish priests must live like the hermits in the Egyptian desert of the first Christian centuries. It does mean that what a priest does in his style of life, his manner of work, and his recreation must always reflect what he *is*. A man is not a priest during parish office hours only. If he is not a priest every hour of every day, if he does not deliberately configure his life so that the iconography of his priesthood is transparent, his concept of priesthood is deficient and his vulnerability to temptation will grow greater.

PRIESTS AND LAY PEOPLE

Which brings us to the tangled and fascinating question of priests and laity. It is striking that that most priestly of priests, Pope John Paul II, is a man whose early experience of the priesthood and later theology of the priesthood were decisively influenced by an intense set of friendships with lay people, young university students whom he served as chaplain and who remained for decades among his closest personal friends. These friendships embody the mutual exchange of gifts between priests and lay people that was envisioned by the Second Vatican Council: openness without confusion of roles or identities, leading to the spiritual enrichment of all concerned. A mature, holy, effective priest need not, indeed cannot, cut himself off from the friendship of lay Catholics if he is to grow humanly, spiritually, and professionally. The difficulties seem to come when there is a confusion of roles and vocations in either or both directions.

Relations between U.S. Catholics and their priests have become much more informal in the past thirty-five years. Much of that has been welcome, indeed salutary, and it has opened up possibilities for spiritual direction, counseling, and sharing of responsibility in parishes and schools that could not have been imagined forty years ago. At the same time, an excessive informality in relations between priests and laity reinforces the powerful, culturally driven tendency in America to think of the priest as a functionary rather than an icon. Lay Catholics then begin to wonder just what the priest is, and so do some priests. A functionally laicized priest and clericalized lay people are not infrequently the unhappy result. The understanding (by all parties) that the priest has pastoral authority over that part of the flock given him to govern is also seriously weakened.

This problem has been exacerbated (even as it is embodied) by another new set of practices, good in themselves, that when taken to extremes unravel the sacramental texture of the priesthood and clericalize the laity: the new roles of lay people in the Church's liturgy, especially the Mass. The most serious problem here has to do with the way holy communion is now distributed in many, if not most, Catholic parishes during Sunday Mass. For more than twenty-five years, the Church has permitted lay people to assist in the distribution of communion as "extraordinary ministers of the Eucharist." "Extraordinary" in this context means "not the ordinary ministers of the Eucharist"—yet that is precisely what lay people have become, while the priest has become the "extraordinary minister" in distributing the sacrament. What was originally intended as a practice to facilitate the distribution of holy communion at Masses with large congregations when only a few priests or deacons were available has now become the norm, and even parishes with several other priests and a deacon or two arrange their liturgy so that the priest celebrating Mass is the only priest involved in the distribution of communion. Lay people now ordinarily remove the preconsecrated hosts from the tabernacle and return to the tabernacle those left over after communion—a practice that is supposed to end in the near future, but whose ubiquity is not going to be significantly reversed without something more than a new set of rules from Rome.

That "something more" is a renewed and deepened understanding of the intimate relationship of the priest to the Eucharist. At the altar, the priest should be most transparently an *alter Christus*, "another Christ." When he speaks the words of eucharistic consecration, he speaks Christ's words of institution at the Last Supper. Similarly, when he offers the body and blood of Christ to his people, he is acting "in the person of Christ," feeding Christ's flock. It is imperative that this rich, sacramental iconography be a visible part of the Church's liturgy. Too frequently it is not, and that has contributed in subtle ways to the crisis of priestly identity in the United States.

When, Sunday after Sunday, nine of the ten people distributing communion at Mass are lay men or women, the signal is being sent that the Catholic community is feeding itself rather than being fed by its priests "in the person of Christ." The not unreasonable inference is then drawn that worship is something we do for each other and for ourselves rather than an obligation we owe to God, whose fulfillment is made possible by the grace of baptism. It is, finally, a short step from that inference to the breakdown of deep faith in the sacramental reality of the body and blood of Christ in the Eucharist, which recent surveys show is a major problem in the Church in the United States.

No serious person proposes a ban on the use of lay men and women as extraordinary ministers of the Eucharist; such a ban would be impractical, given high-density Mass attendance at large parishes, and it would be insulting to the many, many lay men and women who perform this role with reverence. At the same time, the Church must learn, and priests must learn, how to make it clear again that in the Eucharist, the center of Catholic life, the Church is being fed by Christ, in his word and in the person of his priest; the Church is not feeding itself, in some sort of liturgical picnic. Sustained and effective catechesis from the pulpit is one way to begin this small but not inconsequential facet of genuinely Catholic reform. So is a conscious decision, whenever possible, to have multiple priests and deacons distributing communion at Sunday Mass.

PRIESTS AND VOCATIONS TO THE PRIESTHOOD

Is there a shortage of Catholic priests in the United States? Yes. How will that be remedied? Not by dumbing-down the priesthood or abandoning the discipline of clerical celibacy, but by bishops and priests taking vocation recruitment much more seriously

As late as the early 1960s, when there was still an intact Catholic culture in the United States and seminaries were full, it was quite literally impossible for a boy or a young man *not* to think about the possibility of being a priest: The offer was in the air, so to speak, in the daily rhythms of Catholic life and piety. When that intact Catholic culture shattered in the mid-to-late 1960s, too many bishops and priests seemed to assume that the offer was still being made. It wasn't. Other things were on offer, powerfully. It took the Catholic Church in America the better part of two decades to figure out that if a Catholic cultural ambiance wasn't going to make the offer it had better be made by someone else—by priests and bishops.

Dioceses that have grasped this—dioceses in which the bishop talks about vocations to the priesthood at every confirmation and graduation, insists on prayers for vocations at every Mass, has an alert and aggressive vocations office run by a capable priest, and invites interested young men to meet with him regularly to explore the possibilities—have found that the response is a generous one. Young people want to be called to lives of heroism. That truth of the human condition is no less true in our times than in any other. But as a former seminary rector, now a bishop, once said, "A man will give his life for a mystery, but not for a question mark." That is why the dioceses in the United States that have had good results in vocation recruitment in recent decades are also, in the main, dioceses where the bishop and his priests convey a clear, unambiguous sense of the Catholic priest as an icon of the eternal priesthood of Christ.

Priests are indispensable in recruiting vocations to the priesthood. The local bishop can, and must, take the lead, but that leadership will only be effective if it emboldens large numbers of priests in the diocese to put the question to young men regularly: "Have you ever thought that God might be calling you to the priesthood?" Priests who do this regularly find that their own priesthood is enriched. To ask a young man to throw his life away for Christ requires the man asking the question to reflect on the radical quality of his own discipleship. Putting hard questions to others requires a priest to first put hard questions to himself. Proposing a countercultural vocation to a young man requires a priest to think about whether his own life as a priest is sufficiently countercultural.

Thus one path to the reform of the priesthood among those already ordained is for priests to take their roles as vocation recruiters far more seriously.

HANDLING MALFEASANCE

The "answer" to the scandal of clerical sexual abuse is fidelity—a deeper conversion of American priests to Christ. No set of revised clergy personnel policies can induce a revolution of fidelity and deepened conversion among priests. Such policies can, however, help restore the shattered confidence of Catholics in their leadership's ability to come to grips with a crisis and turn it into an opportunity for genuinely Catholic reform.

What would such policies look like?

It is urgently important that this discussion break out of media-generated and, frankly, vulgar categories like "zero tolerance" and "one-strike-and-you're out." The crisis is too serious for such clichés, which usually obscure more than they illuminate. That being said, the following can also be said.

As Pope John Paul II stressed in his address to the U.S. cardinals who were meeting in the Vatican on April 22, 2002, everyone in the Church, and indeed everyone in society, must know that "there is no place in the priesthood and religious life for those who would harm the young." It must be emphasized that while sexual abuse of minors is a serious criminal matter that must be reported to the public authorities it is also, and most fundamentally, a grave sin that cuts to the heart of the truth about the priesthood in the Catholic Church. A priest who sexually abuses the young has so disfigured himself as an icon of the eternal priesthood of Christ that he cannot function any longer as a priest. Period. Therefore, both clerical sexual pedophiles in the strict sense of the term (those who sexually abuse prepubescent children) and those who habitually seduce and abuse minors, heterosexually or, as has been far more prevalent, homosexually, must be dismissed from the clerical state and permanently barred from any future ecclesiastical office. Such sanctions must apply to priests past, present, and future.

The Church has further obligations beyond this drastic remedy. The Church has serious pastoral obligations to the victims of sexual abuse and their families, and must bend every effort to ensure that souls are not permanently maimed by clergy sexual malfeasance. The Church also has the obligation to take effective measures to bring a malfeasant priest to a deeper conversion that enables him to reform his life. The Church's obligations to malfeasant priests do not stop, in other words, with remanding a priest culpable of the sexual abuse of a minor to the public authorities. Priests who fail, even in these hideous ways, remain sons of the Church, and the Church must find ways to restore them to an upright Christian life. While this may well involve therapeutic interventions, it will primarily require spiritual remedies. A catastrophic failure to live celibate chastity is the result of a failure to live holiness of life. If a priest dismissed from the clerical state for predatory sexual abuse is to be saved as a Christian, the Church must assume a responsibility for his deeper conversion as well as his therapy.

Then there is the matter of clerical sexual misconduct, heterosexual or homosexual, with consenting adults. Habitual sexual misconduct with adults must be considered (as indeed it already is in canon law) a sufficient reason for dismissal from the clerical state. This is even more urgently true for homosexual activity by priests with other priests, which must end among diocesan priests and in religious orders if the priesthood in the United States is to be reformed in integrity. Priests themselves have a serious responsibility of fraternal correction and assistance when they know that a brother priest is sinning, heterosexually or homosexually. Priestly fraternity cannot be allowed to be corrupted into a means of ignoring priestly malfeasance, even if that malfeasance involves consensual sex. A priest *is* his brother priest's keeper; a priest who fails to be that, fails in his own priestly responsibility.

That being said, it must also be underscored that the primary responsibility for the discipline of diocesan priests rests with the local bishop, as the primary responsibility for the discipline of priests in religious orders lies with the relevant local superior and the provincial. Those responsibilities are emphatically *not* fulfilled when strict personnel policies are put in place to handle instances of genuine pedophilia and the sexual abuse of minors. Given what prudence requires us to think is a significant incidence of sexual corruption among priests, and given the absolute imperative of reforming the priesthood in order to facilitate the reform of the entire Church, bishops and religious superiors must also take active steps, in light of what has been brought to the surface by the crisis of 2002, to determine whether any priest under their authority is living an unchaste life, heterosexually or homosexually. This may well involve the necessity of personal interviews of every priest under a bishop's or superior's care, in which the priest is reminded of the vow he has taken and then asked, by the bishop or superior, "Are you engaging in any sexual activity whatsoever?" If the answer is yes and involves pedophilia or habitual sexual abuse of minors, the remedies outlined above immediately apply. If the answer is yes, and involves consensual sexual activity of any sort with adults, the priest should be told that he has a week to make up his mind whether he is willing to amend his life, not by degrees, but by immediately ceasing from any sexual activity whatsoever. If he is, every possible spiritual and therapeutic aid should be given him to help him honor that commitment. If he is not, the bishop or superior should inform him that immediate steps will be taken to dismiss him from the clerical state.

What about the priest who falls from grace once, repents, truly amends his life, and lives his celibate chastity in integrity for years or decades? If that sin involves true pedophilia, he should be dismissed from the clerical state because of the gravity of the sin; some sins simply disqualify a man from a further public exercise of the ministry. Indeed, if a true reform of the priesthood took hold in the Church in America, a man conscious of having committed such an offense, even if only once, would feel obliged to request a dismissal from the clerical state. If, on the other hand, the priest's sin involves a consensual sexual relationship with an adult (perhaps under the influence of alcohol), if that sin was not the beginning of a habitual pattern of sexual misconduct, and if the priest has led an exemplary life since, most Catholics would likely say that such a man should not be dismissed from the clerical state. They would be right.

Review boards composed primarily of lay people but also of mature and courageous priests have proven effective in many dioceses in helping the local bishop handle charges of clergy sexual abuse. Such boards will likely become a permanent feature of Catholic life in the United States. If properly constructed and led, they can be a great benefit to the Church. But they cannot be permitted to be the instruments by which the bishop absolves himself of responsibility for priests accused of sexual misconduct. The bishop's responsibility remains, and the bishop's responsibility must be accepted.

More than one American bishop was heard to say, in anticipation of the bishops' semiannual meeting in Dallas in June 2002, that once national clergy personnel norms were adopted and in place the problem of clergy sexual abuse would be "over" and the Church could "put this behind us." Getting such norms implemented is an urgent matter. It is the most profound of mistakes, however, to imagine that the simple fact of strict personnel norms will put the question of the reform of the priesthood in the United States "behind us."

A deeper, more thorough reform, which takes as its goal the reconstitution of priestly identity, is absolutely necessary and must be begun without delay. Bishops who imagine that the Church can go back to business as usual once new national personnel norms are in place are deeply, sadly mistaken. Much, much more is needed in terms of rooting out corruption, enabling today's good priests to be even better priests, and in forming a new generation of priests who, with their older brothers in the ministry, will restore the integrity of the Catholic priesthood in America. National personnel norms to handle instances of clergy sexual abuse are the beginning of the needed reform, not the end. Those who think they are, are deluding themselves.

CHAPTER EIGHT

AGENDA FOR REFORM— THE BISHOPS AND THE VATICAN

THE KEY TO TRANSFORMING the current crisis of the Catholic Church in the United States into an opportunity for genuinely Catholic reform is leadership. If the reform is to be genuinely Catholic and lead to a more intentionally Catholic life throughout the entire Church, it must be led by the bishops. There is no alternative to more intelligent, evangelically assertive, courageous episcopal leadership in the Catholic Church in America.

The bishops must not imagine that they have resolved the

crisis of 2002 by adopting stringent personnel protocols for dealing with clerical sexual abusers and seeing that those protocols are applied in every diocese. The crisis is more than a crisis of clergy sexual abuse, and recent patterns of such abuse have their roots in the deeper crisis—the crisis of fidelity. Unless the crisis of fidelity is vigorously addressed, then even if its surface manifestations are palliated (and the district attorneys and liability lawyers kept at a respectful distance from the chanceries), the diseases that caused them will not have been cured. Reform will be incomplete, future scandals will be inevitable, and the Church in America will not be the vital, active witness to Christian truth that it can and must be.

One of the most distasteful aspects of the crisis of 2002 involved complaints from some bishops who suggested—sometimes subtly, sometimes overtly—that they were being tarred with too much responsibility for the scandal of clergy sexual abuse. This must stop. Without a doubt, critics of the Church from within, and bitter enemies from without, have seized on these scandals to try to destroy the influence of individual bishops and the American hierarchy. But the fact remains that, according to settled Catholic doctrine, the bishops are the responsible leaders of local churches. If a bishop does not understand that he holds primary responsibility for the integrity of Catholic faith in his diocese, which includes responsibility for the discipline of his clergy, he should resign and make way for a man with a clearer conviction about what bishops are and what bishops must do.

The reform of the priesthood—indeed, the reform of the entire Catholic Church in America—will thus require a deep reform of the American episcopate. The Second Vatican Council made a serious effort to lift up the supernatural vocation and real pastoral authority of the local bishop. Yet in a great paradox (and an even greater disappointment), the years following the Council have witnessed too many instances of American bishops incapable of, or unwilling to, live out the unique vocation that is theirs, according to the Council's teaching. Why that happened will be debated and analyzed for a long time. That it happened has been made self-evidently clear by the fact that episcopal misgovernance turned the scandal of clergy sexual abuse into a full-blown crisis for the entire Catholic Church in the United States.

This must be addressed. It must be addressed in a fully Catholic way. The reform of the episcopate, like the reform of the priesthood, cannot mean following any other pattern than the pattern of classic Catholicism: the pattern set by great bishops like Ambrose and Augustine, Athanasius and John Chrysostom, Charles Borromeo and Francis de Sales, Stefan Wyszyński and Karol Wojtyła. That pattern is formed by fidelity wedded to courage and lived in sanctity.

Bishops must come to know, again, that they are genuine vicars of Christ in their own dioceses, not vicars of the pope or vicars of their national conference. Bishops must come to think of themselves, again, as men to whom the Holy Spirit has given the fullness of the sacrament of Holy Orders, not a promotion in a corporate structure. That the word "bishop" derives from the Greek word for "overseer" must never blind the bishop to his basic apostolic responsibilities, which are to be a teacher and a pastor. A bishop, as the Catholic Church understands it, is a successor of the apostles. A brief reading of *Acts* should suffice to demonstrate that the apostles were not managers of the local branch offices of an up-and-coming religious organization trying to find its market niche. They were witnesses to the truth of God revealed in Jesus Christ, to the "ends of the earth" and unto death.

As with the reform of the priesthood, the basic issue is one of the bishop's sacramental identity, and the degree to which the bishops of the United States have made that identity their own in their manner of teaching sanctifying, and governing.

To suggest that genuinely Catholic reform depends on the quality of the Church's bishops is not to reduce the Catholic Church to the episcopate. It is the responsibility of every Catholic to advance the thorough reform of the Church according to the teaching of Vatican II as authoritatively interpreted by Pope John Paul II. That reform will be accomplished most of all by saints, who emerge from every vocational corner of the Catholic world. But bishops are crucial factors in the process of reform. They can initiate reform in their local churches with great effect; or they can impede reform, because of incompetence, incomprehension, or cowardice. With unique authority and from unique pulpits, they can explain to their local churches the origins of the crisis and what must be done to turn crisis into opportunity; or they can retreat into their chanceries, in the conviction that more stringent personnel norms for dealing with clerical sexual abusers will satisfy the criminal law and keep the press at bay. Bishops can be living icons of Christ the Good Shepherd, restoring the flock's confidence in their headship; or they can act as managers rather than pastors, in which case lay confidence will not be restored, the temptation of many Catholics to identify "the Church" exclusively with their local parish will intensify, and the transformation of Catholicism into yet another American denomination will accelerate.

A lot is at stake in whether the bishops of the United States grasp the opportunity that the current crisis has given them.

It is a blessing amid a time of troubles that the Pope who urged the U.S. bishops to their duties in April 2002 was himself one of the most dynamic, effective diocesan bishops of his time. Facing provocations and restrictions from the communist government of Poland that are beyond the imagining of most American ecclesiastical bureaucrats, Karol Wojtyła, as archbishop of Kraków, designed and led one of the most thoughtful and effective implementations of Vatican II in the world, was omnipresent to his priests and people as a father and shepherd, and played a forceful role in Polish intellectual and literary culture. If he could do all these things while an aggressively atheistic state was throwing roadblocks in his path at every turn and working overtime to cajole, persuade, or blackmail his people into apostasy, then surely bishops in far more favorable material and political circumstances can take in hand the reforms that are necessary in the Church in the United States.

Leadership is not impossible in the Church today. Leadership is eminently possible if it is rooted in conviction, and in the courage to be Catholic.

THE SELECTION OF BISHOPS

The key to a long-term reform of the American episcopate commensurate with the great possibilities of the Catholic Church in the United States is a reform in the procedures and criteria by which bishops are selected. The current process is far too ingrown, with a troubled hierarchy having what seems to many an inordinate influence in shaping decisions about who will now be permitted to join the episcopal fraternity. Just as importantly, the criteria by which men are judged to be candidates for the episcopate are too focused on questions of institutional maintenance and personal agreeability and too little focused on zeal and a demonstrated capacity for countercultural leadership.

In the Latin-rite Church in the United States, the pope names diocesan bishops after a process of vetting and nomination that involves the nunciature in Washington, the Congregation for Bishops in Rome, and a variety of informal inputs. In broad consultation (at least theoretically) with bishops, priests, and laity, the nuncio prepares a list of three candidates, a *terna*, for consideration by the Congregation for Bishops, one of the most influential agencies in the Vatican. The nuncio's *terna* is considered by the Congregation's staff, and then by the Congregation's members (all of whom are cardinals or bishops) at their biweekly meeting. The Congregation, through its prefect, then offers a *terna* to the pope for his decision. In some instances, the Congregation is dissatisfied with the nuncio's *terna* and requests further investigation and a revised *terna*. In other instances, the pope is dissatisfied with the Congregation's *terna* and either suggests that the whole process begin again or makes suggestions of his own. (Pope John Paul II, for example, rejected the Congregation's *terna* for New York in 1984, the net result being the surprise appointment of John J. O'Connor as, in John Paul's words, "the archbishop of the capital of the world.")

In actual practice, the consultation process for the nunciature's *terna* is dominated by the bishops and those priests whom they trust or the nuncio trusts—which means that the process of consultation is heavily tilted toward those parts of the clerical bureaucracy that have a vested interest in the status quo. Laity are not involved in this confidential vetting process in any significant way. This is a serious mistake. In assessing a priest's fitness for the office of bishop, lay people can see things that clergy may miss. In any event, common sense suggests that a more broadly consultative process would produce a more balanced assessment of the needs of a diocese and the qualifications of particular candidates. As for confidentiality (which is in fact essential to the integrity of the process), if the Church has survived the indiscretions of the clerical grapevine it need not worry excessively about finding trustworthy and knowledgeable lay Catholics who know how to keep confidences.

The mechanics of the process are of less consequence for deep reform, however, than are the criteria that guide the nomination of bishops. The current criteria are obvious from the form letter that the nuncio sends to those asked to comment on a prospective candidate, in which questions are asked about a priest's character, his fidelity to the Church's teaching, his spiritual life, his habits, and so forth. All of this is unexceptionable. It is also insufficient.

The criteria must be expanded and sharpened so that the selection process takes better account of the cultural climate faced by any man who would teach, govern, and sanctify as a Catholic bishop in the United States in the twenty-first century. That climate is saturated with fears about being considered "intolerant" or "insensitive"—labels readily attached to anyone asserting moral truths that cut against the grain of freedom-(mis)understood-as-license. Moreover, it is a cultural climate deeply influenced by bureaucratic models of governance, which affect everything from the local scout troop and parish council to General Motors, the United Auto Workers, and the Pentagon. It is, in sum, an atmosphere in which it is very easy for a bishop to think of himself as a mitered referee—an episcopal discussion group moderator whose primary responsibility (in addition to fund-raising) is to keep "the dialogue" going and everyone within it reasonably content.

This is not a model of episcopacy that would have made sense to Ambrose or Augustine, Athanasius or John Chrysostom, Francis de Sales or Charles Borromeo. It is also a model of episcopacy that is wholly inadequate to the deep reform of the Catholic Church in the United States according to the mind of the Second Vatican Council. That reform is going to require bishops of vision, determination, and grit, willing to challenge the flaccidity of our culture and the effects of that softness on the life of the Church, which have been made all too painfully evident in the crisis of 2002.

The object of the selection process is to find apostles, men with the convictions necessary to undergird their own courage to be Catholic and the evangelical fire to inspire that courage in others. With that goal in mind, the following should be added to the standard list of questions asked of knowledgeable people about a prospective candidate for the office of bishop:

1. In his life and ministry, does this priest manifest a personal conversion to Jesus Christ and a deliberate choice to abandon everything to follow Christ?

2. Does this priest preach the Gospel with conviction and clarity? Can he make the Church's proposal to those who do not believe? With charity, can he instruct and, if necessary, admonish Catholics who have embraced teachings contrary to the Gospel and the teaching authority of the Church?

3. Has this priest ever been a pastor? Did the parish grow under his leadership? If his primary work has been as a professor in a seminary, did his students flourish under his tutelage?

4. How does this priest celebrate Mass, in concrete and specific terms? Does his liturgical ministry lead his people into a deeper experience of the paschal mystery of Jesus Christ, crucified and risen?

5. How many men have entered the seminary because of this priest's influence? How many women have entered consecrated religious life because of his influence? Does he encourage lay movements of Catholic renewal and the development of popular piety? In sum, is he a man who can call others to holiness of life because he manifests holiness in his own life?

6. Does this priest have the strength of character and personality to make decisions that will be unpopular with other priests and religious, because those decisions are faithful to the Church's teaching and liturgical practice?

7. Is this priest well-read theologically? Does he regard theology as an important part of his vocation? Can he "translate" the best of the Church's theology, ancient and contemporary, into an idiom accessible to his people?

Answers to these questions will help the responsible authorities of the Church determine whether a candidate is a man of conviction and courage. Acknowledging that these are among the important questions to ask will demonstrate that the responsible authorities of the Church recognize the kinds of demands placed on a man who is a twenty-first century Catholic bishop in the United States.

In light of the current crisis, certain other questions must be put to any potential candidate for bishop, and certain people must as a rule be consulted. Those asked to comment on a potential nominee must be explicitly asked whether they are aware of any incident in the candidate's life, involving sexual misconduct or any other impropriety, that would disqualify him for the office of bishop or cause scandal for the Church. Those consulted must include priests who have lived with the potential candidate in a parish or seminary assignment, and at least one active priest, himself of unimpeachable integrity, who was a seminary classmate of the potential candidate. When the nuncio informs a priest that the Holy Father wishes to nominate him as a bishop, the nuncio must explicitly ask the priest whether there is any sexual or other impropriety in his background that makes him unfit for the office; the identical question must be put to a bishop whose transfer to another diocese is being considered, and the same question must be put to other bishops and priests who know the bishop in question well.

The reform of the selection process will also necessitate changes in the minimum age assumed appropriate for a bishop, and in assumptions about what kinds of priests are best qualified for the episcopate.

For some time now, an artificial floor of age fifty seems to have been imposed on nominations for the episcopate in the United States; that is, a man's name simply will not appear on a *terna* unless he has passed his fiftieth birthday. That preference for older bishops, which is understandable in light of some unhappy appointments of much younger men in the years immediately following the Council, must be reversed in light of today's urgent needs and the demographics of the contemporary American priesthood. Those most capable of leading the reform of the Church in the United States in the decades ahead will often be men who are now in their forties, even late thirties—men whose priesthood has been formed in the image of John Paul II and whose episcopate would follow a similar model. Their age should not be held against them as potential bishops, if they have proven themselves effective pastors or seminary educators according to the criteria listed above.

There is also strong historical precedent for appointing younger men as bishops in times of crisis and needed reform. Saint Cyril of Alexandria was a bishop at thirty-six. Saint Ambrose was thirty-four when he was ordained bishop of Milan; his protégé, the great Augustine, was forty-one when he became bishop of Hippo. Two of the great reformer bishops of the post-Reformation period, Saint Francis de Sales and Saint Charles Borromeo, were bishops in their mid-thirties. Stefan Wyszyński was primate of Poland at forty-seven. Men of like caliber are available in the Church in America today.

Then there is the question of intellectuals as bishops. The

Church in the United States has generally been allergic to scholar-bishops. And while the record of some academics-turned-bishops in Europe in the past forty years has been discouraging, there is the powerful counter-example of John Paul II, a true scholar-bishop, to conjure with. In the United States today there are theologians, philosophers, and historians, proven effective as teachers and spiritual directors, who would make exemplary bishops. Their doctorates and their scholarly careers should not be considered impediments to their episcopal ordination.

A new assessment of the fitness of career Church bureaucrats for the episcopacy is also long overdue. There is, arguably, too much raillery about Church bureaucracy today; priests who work in chancery offices or the national bishops' conference can be entirely admirable people. Yet eighty years after sociologist Max Weber dissected the character of bureaucracies, it should also be clear that the typical bureaucratic cast of mind—which emphasizes efficient management and damage-control, and almost always prefers amelioration to necessary confrontation—can be in serious tension with the bishop's duty to teach, govern, and sanctify. That much, at least, should have been learned from the fiascos of episcopal misgovernance that have helped turn clerical scandal into Church-wide crisis.

That Anthony O'Connell was appointed a bishop after his superiors knew that he had been a principal in a sexual molestation lawsuit—and that he was then reassigned, years later, as the bishop of a diocese that had just been rocked by its own bishop's sexual misconduct—demonstrates beyond cavil that something is seriously broken in the process by which bishops are selected. The process must be fixed, quickly. This, fortunately, is something the Holy See can do, after appropriate consultations with the Congregation for Bishops, by instruction to the nuncio. Those consultations and the appropriate instructions about new criteria should not be delayed.

THE NATIONAL CONFERENCE

While the structure of the U.S. bishops' national conference was streamlined recently so that what had been a bureaucratic dyad—the National Conference of Catholic Bishops and its public policy agency, the United States Catholic Conference—has been merged into a single entity, the U.S. Conference of Catholic Bishops, the basic cast of mind of the conference and its operating procedures remain intact. After Vatican II, the original design of the bishops' national operation was led by Cardinal John Dearden of Detroit, then the conference president, who chose the management-consultant firm of Booz-Allen Hamilton to advise the bishops on how they should do their corporate business. (Cardinal Dearden was reportedly impressed by the work that firm had done in restructuring the management of the auto industry, but that is another story.) Dearden and the man he chose as the first post–Vatican II conference general secretary, Joseph

Bernardin (subsequently archbishop of Cincinnati and still later cardinal archbishop of Chicago), took the consultants' plan and imbued the conference's proceedings with a consensus model of decision-making. Those atmospherics are redolent in the bishops' ten-year-old, $29 million state-of-the-art office complex in Washington, D.C., near the campus of the Catholic University of America, and in the bishops' semi-annual meetings, which are typically held in large hotels. There is little reason to think that the atmospherics have been changed by the change to a single corporate entity, the USCCB.

There is, however, ample reason to think that the crisis of 2002 has exposed the grave insufficiencies of both the process and the atmospherics of the bishops' conference.

The leadership of the USCCB and the conference's highly influential staff pride themselves on the "consensus" model of decision-making and on the process that gives shape to the "consensus." The model and the process are, to put it charitably, deficient. The inability of the national conference to persuade every diocese in the country to adopt strict personnel protocols for dealing with clergy sexual abuse throughout the 1990s is a case in point. But that failure was presaged by many others: the lengthy delays in getting national norms with real traction for implementing *Ex Corde Ecclesiae*, the 1990 apostolic constitution on the Catholic identity of Catholic universities; the bishops' endless thrashings with liturgical translations; the weaknesses in the seminary visitations of the 1980s; the fiasco of the finally abandoned proposed pastoral letter on women's concerns; a highly controversial 1997 letter to Catholic parents on homosexual children, which seemed to begin from the assumption that parents were bigots who required instruction in the fine points of contemporary psychological theory.

At the practical level, one problem is that the bishops' semi-annual meetings are conducted according to *Robert's Rules of Order* (complete with parliamentarian); *Robert's* is an admirable tool in many respects, but its ubiquity in the bishops' deliberations may well have led to a confusion between a debate conducted according to its methods, and genuine episcopal discernment and deliberation. The ways the bishops' discussions are structured also mitigates against real exchange. Bishops are slotted to speak in terse statements (their time being governed by traffic lights on the dais), and the statements frequently have nothing to do with what preceded them. These are not the circumstances in which real conversation—much less real confrontation, if necessary—can take place. These problems are further exacerbated by the bishops' decision to do most of their business in full view of the press and TV cameras, with only the most sensitive matters reserved for executive session. The instinct for openness is perhaps admirable, but it, too, creates circumstances that mitigate against real exchange. (The working sessions of Vatican II, for example, were not open to the press, and while no one would cite Vatican II's procedures as a model of parliamentary debate, those procedures and the Council's restriction of press access to its substantive discussions at least created the circumstances in which hard truths could be told if necessary, because the world's bishops were speaking to each other and not to NBC or the BBC.)

Whatever its accomplishments in promoting a sense of episcopal fraternity and in coordinating certain worthwhile projects, the functioning of the bishops' conference over the past thirty-five years has also worked to reinforce the culturally driven tendency to remake the Catholic Church in the United States into another American denomination. One crucial aspect of that makeover (a dynamic also evident in virtually every liberal Protestant denomination in America since World War II) is the transformation of the charism of religious leadership into the "skill set" of bureaucratic managership. That has all too frequently happened in the self-understanding of American bishops, a process that the conference has reinforced by its *modus operandi*. The conference has rewarded those bishops who "get along" with leadership positions; it has reinforced the temptation of bishops to think of themselves primarily as conversation-moderating consensus-builders and managers, rather than apostles; it has not demonstrated an ability to come to grips effectively with the culture of dissent on Catholic campuses, in seminaries, and in diocesan offices. On the contrary, it has helped reinforce the episcopal instinct to think of "faithful dissent" as something that can be "managed." That this has been done in the name of a Council that laid renewed emphasis on the evangelical nature of the Church and the sacramental distinctiveness of the local bishop is beyond ironic; it is tragic.

How what is broken in the USCCB might be fixed is beyond the scope of this small book. That serious rethinking and restructuring is imperative was evident from the title of an admiring study of the conference published in 1993 by Father Thomas Reese, S.J.: *A Flock of Shepherds*. When shepherds become flocks, shepherds become sheep, and something in the nature of a shepherd is gravely damaged.

CHANGES IN ROME

The crisis of 2002 has also made it abundantly clear that there are things that require repair in the processes by which the Vatican gathers information, communicates its thinking and concerns, and interacts with the American bishops.

The information flow from the nunciature in Washington to the Holy See has been manifestly inadequate and must be addressed. This will require the nuncio and his staff to consult far more widely within the Catholic Church in the United States in order to be able to transmit a textured picture of the American situation to Rome, and to ensure that the Holy See—and the Pope—are fully aware of potential crises before they explode.

The Vatican's own information-sharing processes are also in need of repair. The sluggish reaction to the unfolding Catholic crisis in the United States in the early months of

2002 was due in part to the lack of a coordinated information flow among the relevant dicasteries of the Roman Curia. The information coming in from the United States was inadequate, but what information was available was not adequately circulated, with the result that appropriate interdepartmental measures to address the unfolding crisis were late in coming.

The fiasco of the press conference that concluded the U.S. cardinals' meeting on April 23, 2002, was another demonstration of an inadequate communications strategy in the Vatican. So was the lack of coordination among heads of Vatican offices who addressed the crisis in the wake of that meeting. Within two weeks of the Pope's addressing the crisis of clergy sexual abuse in uncompromising and forthright terms, locating its roots in the culture of dissent and challenging everyone in the U.S. Church to a deeper fidelity, the President of the Pontifical Council for the Interpretation of Legislative Texts opined, in a lecture in Milan, that a "correct legal view" of the situation would be adequate in "reestablishing serenity in so many disturbed spirits." For various reasons, including inadequate coordination among curial departments, Archbishop Julián Herranz did not seem to realize that those "disturbed spirits" were in fact angry, faithful Catholics, scandalized by clerical sexual abuse and further scandalized by the evident incapacity of some bishops to deal with the problem. Archbishop Herranz's use of phrases like "emotional wave of public clamor" and "easy emotions and superficial impressions," coupled with his warnings about churchmen being unduly "influenced by the media impact of these painful cases," also suggested a man who, whatever his good intentions, was woefully ill-informed about the realities of the situation. Archbishop Herranz stated in his lecture that he was speaking in a private, rather than official, capacity; that only confirmed the impression that the Holy Father's view of the nature of the problem simply wasn't being communicated to some of his closest collaborators, who should have been expected to reinforce the Pope's message, not undercut it.

It is surely not beyond the capacity of the Holy See to take measures to ensure that all of its senior officials are speaking off the same script as the Pope. This is not simply good communications strategy; it is crucial to the integrity of the Church's message.

Beyond these important matters of information flow, curial coordination, and communications strategy, however, lies an even harder set of questions that the Church's authorities in Rome must address: When has a bishop, by personal misconduct, malfeasance in disciplining his clergy, unorthodox teaching, or manifest incompetence in effecting needed reforms lost the capacity to govern his diocese according to the mind of the Church? What are the criteria by which the Church's highest authorities would make such a judgment? How can such decisions be made, and remedies put immediately into place, in such a way that the Church is not held hostage to hostile media attacks on a local bishop, or campaigns mounted by the culture of dissent, both of which may be motivated by something other than a passionate concern for Catholic doctrine and ecclesiastical discipline?

These will not be easy questions to answer. But they must be faced and addressed, and answers must be found. For good reasons—a profound respect for the office of bishop and for the legitimate prerogatives of the local bishop—as well as for reasons of institutional inertia and nervousness about further scandal, it is very difficult for the authorities in Rome to recognize that far more scandal is created by malfeasant or incompetent bishops than by replacing them. Yet that recognition must come.

There is little doubt that such replacements will be necessary in the future, including the short-term future. The question is how such difficult steps can be taken without doing further damage to the Church's integrity. For the past 200 years, the Catholic Church has worked diligently to disentangle the appointment of bishops from the machinations of secular governments who claimed a leading role in that process—a venerable practice that, under nineteenth and twentieth century conditions, was compromising the integrity of the Church's ministry. Having successfully broken free of the embrace of the state in nominating bishops, the Church cannot mortgage its freedom to select its bishops to popular plebiscites. Contrary to the culture of dissent, Rome's leading role in appointing bishops has enlarged the Church's freedom of action. Protecting that accomplishment is another reason why the Vatican has been reluctant to consider the replacement of bishops under the pressures of public scandal. What the Holy See must understand now is that scandals exacerbated by episcopal incompetence or irresponsibility threaten the very freedom of action the Vatican urgently wishes to protect.

That, and not appeasing popular opinion, is why the question of replacing malfeasant, incompetent, or unorthodox bishops must be squarely faced. And that is also why criteria for determining when a bishop has lost the capacity to govern—to be the good shepherd he has been ordained to be—must be devised. Such criteria are badly needed, for such judgments are going to have to be made. In dealing with these very difficult questions, criteria that reflect the Church's doctrinal convictions and its theologically grounded disciplinary concerns are the best defense against succumbing to campaigns for episcopal resignations mounted by the culture of dissent in effective cooperation with hostile elements in the media.

The episcopate in the United States has a grave responsibility for its own reform. So does the Vatican. Both must now face that responsibility if crisis is to become opportunity, the evangelical mission of the Church advanced, and the bright promise of Vatican II redeemed.

CHAPTER NINE

FROM CRISIS
TO REFORM

OROTHY DAY, COFOUNDER of the Catholic Worker movement, was particularly fond of a challenge to fidelity and courage once posed by Pope Pius XI. The challenge took the form of an invitation to prayer: "Let us thank God that he makes us live among the present problems. It is no longer permitted to anyone to be mediocre." Indeed, it is not. Christian excellence, deeper conformity to Christ, is what is required of everyone in the Catholic Church who is committed to transforming the crisis of clergy sexual abuse and episcopal misgovernance into genuinely Catholic reform.

The crisis of 2002 is, in truth, a metaphor for the entire post-Vatican II Catholic situation. Is Catholic reform a matter of accommodation to the spirit of the age, and specifically to the claims of the sexual revolution? Or is Catholic reform a matter of recovering and developing the Church's essential "form," the truths given it by Christ, which include moral truths about the ways in which human beings truly flourish?

Reform without reference to "form" is mere accommodation. The Second Vatican Council grew out of a great theological effort aimed at recovering and developing the Church's originating "form": the *ressourcement* movement, which sought to revitalize the Church's essential "form" for our time by returning to the great sources of Christian wisdom in Scripture, the Church fathers of the first millennium, and the medieval theological masters. That rediscovery, the *ressourcement* theologians believed, would then lead to a truly Catholic *aggiornamento* (updating) of the Church's life and thought. There could be no *aggiornamento* without *ressourcement*—no reform without form.

THE LAST HURRAH

The culture of dissent, which bears a heavy weight of responsibility for creating the ecclesiastical conditions from which the present Catholic crisis emerged, refuses to grasp this essential point. Its sense of the essential "form" of Catholicism has been severely weakened. Because of that, what it means by "reform" is better described as deconstruction. What the culture of dissent imagines as reform is, in fact, Catholic Lite.

The Lite Brigade, however, has had its moment. That moment is past. One of the sadder things about the crisis of 2002 was to watch so many of the aging veterans of the Lite Brigade, whose misconceived proposals and institutional agitations had done so much to make the crisis possible, returning to the airwaves and the op-ed pages for that unexpected and quintessentially American opportunity—the second chance. They seemed reinvigorated, jaunty, utterly insouciant about any possible responsibility they might bear for the crisis. It was, in a word, pathetic.

The pontificate of John Paul II has been very difficult for the culture of dissent. Karol Wojtyła was exactly what the Lite Brigade wanted as pope in 1978: a modern European intellectual, widely traveled, multilingual, happy and confident, with extensive pastoral experience and terrific public presence. Within months, it became evident that the Lite Brigade, having gotten what it wanted, now rued the day when it had made its wish. So the attack on John Paul II as a man out-of-step with modernity began. The truth of the matter is that John Paul II is the first truly modern pope, in the sense of a pope with a thoroughly modern intellectual formation. What he had, though, was a very different reading of modernity than the Lite Brigade. He did not propose to surrender to modernity. He proposed to convert it.

Karol Wojtyła had been convinced since the Second World War that the crisis of world civilization that had turned the twentieth century into a slaughterhouse was a crisis of humanism—a crisis caused by desperately defective ideas about the human person, human origins, human history, and human destiny. A close friend of the great French *ressourcement* theologian, Henri de Lubac, S. J., Wojtyła agreed with Father de Lubac's argument that the "drama of atheistic humanism" had led, inexorably, to the Gulag, to Auschwitz, and to the debilitating utilitarianism that reduces human beings to materials for others' manipulation. Recognizing that, the Church's culture-forming task was to help rescue the humanistic project by proposing an alternative to atheistic humanism: *Christian* humanism, based on the conviction that Jesus Christ reveals both the face of the merciful Father and the true meaning of our lives. That, Wojtyła proposed, is what the Second Vatican Council should be about. And that is what the pontificate of John Paul II has been about.

The Lite Brigade has missed all of this. The dialogue it imagines with modernity is in fact a monologue. There is little in Catholic Lite theology that poses a serious countercultural challenge to the spirit of the age. Catholic Lite is a soft Catholicism, understanding and sympathetic. Being understanding and sympathetic are, of course, virtues. But as G. K. Chesterton pointed out long ago, the world is filled with old Christian virtues "gone mad." When a great religious tradition is profoundly challenged, as Christianity is by modernity, more than vices are set loose in the world, Chesterton wrote: "The virtues are let loose also; and the virtues wander more wildly, and the virtues do more terrible damage." That is precisely what has happened in the culture of dissent. Virtues have gone mad, and one result has been the double-edged crisis of clergy sexual abuse and episcopal irresponsibility. That crisis can only be addressed by a harder, more brilliant form of Catholicism—a Catholicism formed, like a diamond, under intense pressure, but all the more beautiful and shatterproof for that.

The crisis of 2002 has many facets. One of them is that it marked the last hurrah of the Catholic Lite Brigade. Yes, the Lite Brigade still holds the commanding heights of Catholicism's most prestigious intellectual institutions, protected from its own intellectual sterility by the tenure system. But even there, the crumbling has begun. A younger generation of scholars is not interested in Catholic Lite. Young men and women, formed in the image of John Paul II and joyfully living the Catholic sexual ethic, are filling graduate departments of theology and philosophy at Catholic universities where, as recently as ten years ago, the Lite Brigade was impregnable. These younger scholars are the future. The members of the Lite Brigade may still be good for TV sound bites and newspaper op-ed pieces, in part because the American media can't break itself of the habit of writing the "man bites dog" story of Catholic dissent. But the Lite Brigade is aging. It is not producing a new generation formed intellectually in its image. And the results of its promotion of "faithful dissent" are now on display, in clerical sexual scandals and irresponsible episcopal leadership. The game is over.

THE IRON LAW

The Catholic crisis of 2002 is also a powerful reminder of the Iron Law of Christianity and Modernity: Christian communities that maintain their doctrinal identity and moral boundaries flourish in the modern world; Christian communities that fudge doctrine and morals decay. Contrary to much popular wisdom, the Christian movement is flourishing throughout the world. And in all instances, without exception, it is the Christian communities that eschew Lite approaches to doctrine and morals that are growing.

The Iron Law emphatically does not require the Catholic Church to retreat into an intellectual bunker. The Church is in the world for the world, even if the Church must often challenge the world's understanding of what is true and good. A Catholic Church that pulls up the drawbridges, shutters its windows, bolts the doors, and hunkers down until the storms blow over and the barbarians retreat back into the forest is a Church that is failing in its evangelical mission. In those circumstances, the Church loses and so does the world.

Taking the Iron Law seriously, however, requires that the dialogue with modernity be a genuinely two-way conversation, in which it is understood that the wisdom of the Christian tradition, a rich patrimony built up over two millennia, has things to say—important things, that modernity ignores at its peril. The question of freedom comes immediately to mind. Freedom untethered from moral truth eventually and inevitably becomes self-cannibalizing. When freedom becomes mere license, chaos inexorably follows. And since human beings cannot live in chaos, men and women, faced with the choice between chaos and chains, will ask for chains. Freedom then dies. The classic Catholic conviction that freedom is not a matter of doing what we like, but rather of having the right to do what we ought, is essential if the modern quest for freedom is not going to decompose into new forms of authoritarianism. The classic Catholic conviction that freedom involves growth into the capacity to choose the good as a matter of habit is essential if freedom is not to decay into a new form of self-imposed slavery—the slavery of bondage to the imperial, self-constituting Self. Clerical sexual predators are men enslaved in precisely that way. The wreckage they have wrought, in individual lives and in the Church as a community, is an object lesson in the imperative of a broader, more critical dialogue between the Church and modernity than has been envisioned by the culture of dissent. It has been a lesson long in coming. Its meaning must now be learned.

THE SECOND SORROWFUL MYSTERY

The twenty decades of the rosary include four cycles of meditations on the life of Christ: the joyful mysteries (having to do with the Christmas story and Christ's early life); the luminous mysteries (having to do with the public life of Jesus); the sorrowful mysteries (involving Christ's passion and death); and the glorious mysteries (the resurrection and its effects in the early Church). The second sorrowful mystery is the scourging of Christ at the pillar, recounted in all four gospel accounts of the passion.

The Church cannot but live the life of the Church's divine Master. Thus the scourging at the pillar is an apt metaphor for the Church's situation in America during the crisis of 2002. The Catholic Church has been scourged, mocked, beaten, and humiliated. The scourging has been worse, and the humiliation has been more intense, because so much of it has been due to the wickedness and irresponsibility of the Church's sons, including its ordained ministers.

It is essential for all those committed to living the fullness of Catholic truth to recognize that the humiliation will very likely continue for awhile. It must be borne. That humiliation will inevitably shape the way faithful Catholics think about the Church. It is one thing, and a true thing, to say that the Catholic Church is a Church of sinners, that even the dissolution of some Renaissance popes couldn't destroy the Church, that the Church has already passed through, and been strengthened by, many periods of suffering and purgation. It is another thing to experience corruption and the humiliation that accompanies it day in and day out. No Catholic in the United States today, however old, has ever gone through such an experience before. The effects of that humiliation cannot be completely foreseen, but that there will be effects, and sometimes troubling effects, is a certainty.

That is why Catholics in the United States must pray and reflect on the mystery of the cross. A popular ditty of the immediate post-Vatican II years had it that "We are resurrection people, and alleluia is our song!" True enough. But before the resurrection came the cross and the humiliation and sense of abandonment that comes from being nailed to the cross. It is not masochism but sound Christian doctrine to recognize that one lesson of the crisis of 2002 is that Catholics in the United States must embrace the cross in the sure hope that, as it did almost two millennia ago, Easter will follow Good Friday.

Christians believe that the worst in human history has already happened. It happened on Good Friday, when humanity nailed the Son of God to the cross ". . .and there was darkness all over the earth" [*Matthew* 27.45]. The answer to that was given three days later when the light shown across the land again, indeed shone as it had never shone before. That the cross leads to the resurrection is an article of faith. So is the hard truth that the road to Easter glory always runs through Calvary. That is why the Church in the United States must not shy away from the particular Calvary that is the crisis of clergy sexual abuse and episcopal misgovernance. The evils that led to these acts of betrayal must be understood for what they are. They must be exorcised from the Church. That is the unavoidable purgation that must precede the resurrection.

WHOSE CHURCH?

In March 2002, Betsy Conway, a Sister of St. Joseph in the Archdiocese of Boston, was quoted by syndicated columnist Michael Kelly as saying, "This is our Church, all of us, and we need to take it back." Michael Kelly agreed. Both he and Sister Betsy are mistaken.

The Church is Christ's, not ours. It was not created by us, or by our Christian ancestors, or by the donors to the diocesan annual fund, but by Jesus Christ—a point the Lord made abundantly clear himself in the gospels: "You did not choose me, but I chose you" [*John* 15.16]. As one Jesuit priest, a close student and sharp critic of the corruptions of his own community, wrote to friends in response to Kelly's column, "The Church is not ours to take back because it never belonged to us, and the instant we make it 'our own' we are damned. No merely human institution, no matter how perfectly pure and gutsy and dutiful its members, can take away even a venial sin. That is the point St. Paul takes sixteen chapters to get across to the Romans."

A recently ordained priest preaching during the first weeks of the crisis recounted a story of St. Francis of Assisi. In Francis's time, the thirteenth century, clerical sexual morality was abysmal and lay sexual morality was even worse. Once, one of his brother Franciscans, a man very concerned about scandal, came up to him and asked, "Brother Francis, what would you do if you knew that the priest celebrating Mass had three concubines?" Francis replied, "When it came time for holy communion, I would go to receive the sacred body of my Lord from the priest's anointed hands." Francis of Assisi (for all the saccharine sweetness of *Brother Sun, Sister Moon,* and similar cinematic confections) was no naif. In the last years of his life he bore the stigmata, the wounds of the crucified Christ, in his own flesh. His answer to his disturbed Franciscan brother was theologically orthodox and deeply insightful: It is Christ's Church, and it celebrates the sacraments through Christ's grace. That is terribly important to remember when, as must happen, the people of the Church call the priests and bishops of the Church to account for their stewardship. The people of the Church have a duty to make that call to accountability, and to make sure that it is heard. The people of the Church must always remember, though, that it is Christ's Church, not ours.

Priests and bishops have been much on the minds of U.S. Catholics during the crisis, but Catholics would be very mistaken if they thought that this crisis of fidelity doesn't have something to do with all of us. Christ, whose Church it is, has a particular way of dealing with times of scandal and reform: Through the Holy Spirit, Christ deals with the failings of the Church's sons and daughters by raising up saints to renew the Church in the fullness of Catholic truth.

That means that the only adequate response to the crisis of 2002 is the response that is always called for when the Church is bottoming out. The call to holiness must be lived more intensely by every member of the Church, in whatever state of life. *Everyone.* The crisis of 2002 is, in this respect, like every other crisis in the Church's history. It is a crisis caused by an insufficiency of saints. That is a wake-up call for every Catholic—a call not to "take back" what is not ours to begin with, but to live holier lives.

THE GREAT ADVENTURE

Change is needed in the self-understanding and discipline of the Catholic clergy. The Church badly needs episcopal leadership confident in its headship and prepared to do what must be done to transform crisis into evangelical opportunity. By the same token, Catholics must understand that the path from scandal to reform and from crisis to opportunity is not primarily one of institutional repair. What is broken must be fixed. But there is so much more to be fixed than can be fixed by institutional reforms alone, important as they are.

The path from crisis to reform is the path along which the entire Church rediscovers the great adventure of fidelity and Catholic orthodoxy. Catholic Lite fails because it is wrong; Catholic Lite also fails because it is boring. The romance of orthodoxy is, in fact, the romance of the world. For if what the Church teaches is not just the truth about the Church's story but the truth about the world's story, then to be an orthodox Catholic, thinking with the mind of the Church and living in service to others because of one's Catholic convictions, is to help the world achieve its true destiny.

That is a great adventure. There is nothing dull or boring about the great adventure of orthodoxy. It is a journey full of mountains, deserts, and storms. Oftentimes it draws from us more than we imagine to be within us—and then, when we think we have reached the end of our resources, we find that the Holy Spirit has replenished the well of our courage, which turns out to be deeper, and its water more sweet, than we could have imagined.

Living the adventure of orthodoxy is the only answer to the crisis of fidelity that *is* the crisis of the Catholic Church in the United States read in its true depth. Rediscovering the courage to be Catholic is the way in which all the people of the Church—bishops, priests, laity—will transform scandal into reform, and crisis into opportunity.

That can happen. It will happen. The purification through which the Church is going must have been intended by God for a purpose. That purpose is the renovation of the Church according to the teaching of the Second Vatican Council. Without flinching from the facts of scandal and malfeasance or the humiliation that attends them, every Catholic committed to truly Catholic reform can say, with Pope Pius XI and Dorothy Day, "Let us thank God that he makes us live among the present problems. It is no longer permitted to anyone to be mediocre."

AFTERWORD TO THE PAPERBACK EDITION

Another parable he put before them saying, "The kingdom of heaven may be compared to a man who sowed good seed in his field; but while men were sleeping, his enemy came and sowed weeds among the wheat, and went away. So when the plants came up and bore grain, then the weeds appeared also. And the servants of the householder came and said to him, 'Sir, did you not sow good seed in your field? How then has it weeds?' He said to them, 'An enemy has done this.' The servants said to him, 'Then do you want us to go and gather them?' But he said, 'No; lest in gathering the weeds you root up the wheat along with them. Let both grow together until the harvest; and at harvest time I will tell the reapers, Gather the weeds first and bind them in bundles to be burned, but gather the wheat into my barn."'

MATTHEW 13.24–30

{ 233 }

This familiar gospel story describes the Church at any moment in its history, this side of history's consummation in the Kingdom of God. The Church was wheat and weeds in those heady first weeks after Pentecost when, amid vibrant evangelization and rapid expansion, Ananias and Sapphira lied to Peter and were struck dead at his feet. The Church was wheat and weeds in Renaissance Italy, when reformers contested with the Borgia pope, Alexander VI, for the soul of Catholicism. The Church was wheat and weeds in sixteenth century England, when every English bishop but one truckled to Henry VIII's claim to be "Supreme Governor" of the Church. The Church was wheat and weeds in modern America when too many priests sexually abused those entrusted to their care and too few bishops acted effectively to defend and promote priestly chastity—the twin and inseparable problems that created the "crisis" referred to in the subtitle of this book.

And the Church is wheat and weeds today, two years after the beginning of what many, following the apt phrase of Father Richard John Neuhaus, came to call the Long Lent of 2002.

It would be difficult to argue that, over the past two years, the Catholic Church in America has boldly seized the opportunity to turn this crisis into a moment of authentic Catholic reform. A stable framework in Church law has been established for dealing with accusations of sexual abuse by priests. But the framework itself is not without problems, and in any case legal remedies, however important, cannot resolve the deeper issues involved in this crisis: the nature of the priesthood and the episcopate, the truths of Catholic sexual ethics, the Second Vatican Council's teaching on the Church as a "communion" of disciples formed by an authoritative tradition. These issues are theological, not legal, in character. Revisions in Church law and management practice can help the Church cope more effectively with manifestations of disease in the Body of Christ; legal and managerial change can neither address the underlying pathologies nor promote robust ecclesial health.

Reduced to essentials, my argument in *The Courage To Be Catholic* was that the Long Lent of 2002 was the product of a damaged Church ecology: the twin aspects of the crisis—sexually abusive priests and bishops unable or unwilling to deal with those priests—were both the result of damage done to the Catholic environment in the United States over several decades. Many toxins damaged the ecology of U.S. Catholicism, including toxins from the broader cultural environment in which the Church lives. The most potent toxin, however, was homegrown—a "culture of dissent" which proposed that the Church's teaching authority taught falsehoods on contested questions of sexual morality, abortion, homosexuality, and the ordination of women to the priesthood. This "culture of dissent," I suggested, had done serious damage to the idea of the priesthood and the idea of the episcopate in the Church in the United States. Defective ideas, as ever, had consequences in behaviors and institutional practices. The damage those defective ideas did to the priesthood helped create conditions in which incidents of sexual abuse multiplied; the damage they did to the episcopate helped create circumstances in which individual bishops, and the bishops' conference as a whole, found it difficult to come to grips with the problems of undisciplined, unchaste, and abusive clergy.

Damaged ecosystems produce mutations and lethal diseases. The grossest manifestations of ecological damage to the fabric of Catholic life in the United States will be dealt with by the new legal norms adopted by the U.S. bishops (although not, alas, without creating other problems, including new difficulties in the relationship between priests and bishops). But unless the deeper ecological problems that led to these mutations and diseases are forthrightly and systematically addressed, crisis-as-cataclysm will not become crisis-as-opportunity in the Catholic Church in the United States. Some bishops are addressing these deeper problems in their dioceses. At the national level, proposals for a new forum in which the bishops of the United States could corporately recommit themselves to authentic Catholic teaching on sexual morality, priestly and episcopal character, and celibacy are a welcome sign of recognition that the current episcopal conference structure is not accelerating, and in some instances may be slowing down, authentic Catholic reform. Yet it would be overly sanguine to suggest that there has been widespread acceptance by the bishops of the United States of a comprehensive agenda for reform that would complete the great work of the Second Vatican Council by addressing the failures to implement the Council's authentic teaching that helped create the Long Lent of 2002.

The leaders of the bishops' conference and senior conference staff have denied that there is any linkage between the "culture of dissent" and the crisis of 2002—just as they have continued to use clinical terms like "ephebophilia" rather than confront hard facts about the homosexual abuse of teenage boys and young men by clergy. There has been no systematic examination of the vocation recruitment process; nor has there been progress toward a new and vigorous examination of American seminaries, to complete the seminary reform process begun in the late 1980s. Some bishops still seem more comfortable with the language of "boundary violations" than with the language of sin and grace, conversion and repentance and reconciliation. The "triumph of the therapeutic," in which psychology regularly trumps moral theology, seems to have continued virtually unchecked; some "child-protection" programs proposed for U.S. dioceses deal almost exclusively with the mechanics of human sexuality, while avoiding the deeper questions of love, chastity, and the nobility of marriage that set the framework for Catholic teaching about sexual love and its place within the orders of creation and redemption. A devoutly Catholic journalist, thinking about all this, told me that it seemed as if the bishops were afraid of their own teaching. I suggested that he not paint the American episcopate with too broad a brush; but I couldn't tell him that he was wrong about some bishops, either.

The bishops have also failed to regain the habit—an old-fashioned word in moral philosophy for "virtue"—of fraternal correction. The taboo against confronting a brother bishop in cases of irresponsible leadership remains firmly in place, even if the question is fraternal correction behind the closed doors of an executive session of the bishops' conference. Asked why a public dissenter from the Church's teaching on abortion had been appointed to the bishops' own lay review board studying the crisis of 2002, conference leaders replied that the orthodoxy of the man in question had been confirmed by his local bishop, and that no bishop would ever challenge another bishop's judgment on such a matter. To which one can only say, why not? Augustine surely would have challenged his brother bishop's judgment. So would Charles Borromeo.

Some bishops complain that criticism of them has gone too far. No doubt some critics have been extreme. But everything written about the episcopate here is in defense of the office of bishop as crucial for the life of the Church and its authentic reform. Moreover, bishops who make complaints about criticism their primary lens for reading the signs of the times risk missing a troubling dynamic in Catholic life today, two years after the crisis of 2002 broke in public. For the most disturbing emotional afterburn of the Long Lent of 2002 that I detect among dedicated, loyal Catholics is a deep frustration, bordering on anger, with what is perceived to be a continuing failure of episcopal leadership. This is very dangerous—not because it will eventually lead to a mass exodus from the Church, but because such frustrations and angers, unaddressed, will reinforce in the Catholic Church the powerful American impulse toward congregational religion. If Catholics retreat into the parishes, renewal movements, or retreat centers that they know and trust, effectively cutting themselves off from the life of the diocese or the universal Church, the cause of authentic Catholic reform is likely to be further impeded.

Catholics intuitively understand that the local bishop's task, and the national bishops' conference's task, is not to define the 50-yard line of Catholic life, between what are assumed to be two end zones of extremist views. As Pope John Paul II underscored in *Pastores Gregis* [The Shepherds of the Flock], his October 2003 apostolic exhortation on the ministry of bishop in the 21st century, the bishop's first task is to be a forthright teacher and promoter of authentic Catholic doctrine. Which, to continue the football imagery, means that the bishop's task is not to find, much less occupy, the 50-yard line between authentic doctrine and the culture of dissent. Many of the younger and newer members of the U.S. bishops' conference understand that. As their numbers increase, the opportunities for the bishops becoming, as a body, the primary leaders of authentic Catholic reform will also increase. This suggests, in turn, that the single most crucial factor in turning crisis-as-cataclysm into crisis-as-opportunity in the Catholic Church in the United States is a refined set of criteria for the selection of bishops, criteria based on the understanding that a "pastoral" bishop is, first and foremost, a bishop who can teach the fullness of Catholic truth in an inviting, compelling way.

Among the weeds that have become more visible since this book was first published, three in particular are worth mentioning.

The Long Lent of 2002 has had a bad effect on Church–state relations in the United States. From Massachusetts to Arizona and at many point between, local authorities, including state attorneys general and county prosecutors, are claiming a role in the internal governance of the Catholic Church that should disturb anyone committed to religious freedom. Yes, the opening to that assertion of state power over Catholic life has come about because of irresponsible Catholic leadership. But that simply reinforces the point made above, that the bishops themselves must take responsibility for confronting and dealing with malfeasance or incompetence among their brother bishops. If they don't, state authorities will do it for them. This will inevitably damage the liberty of the Church. It will also damage democracy and the cause of limited, constitutional government.

Then there is the Church's new position in the press. I argued above, and I repeat here, that the Catholic crisis that continues today is the Church's crisis, not an invention of the media. Yet over the past two years, something seems to have changed, something not unlike what changed in the press's default position vis-à-vis government after Watergate. Since Watergate, the reigning assumption among many reporters and editors has been that "they" are lying, or at the very least "spinning." The presumption of good faith is no longer granted to public officials, and a kind of unwritten Napoleonic code—you're guilty until you prove yourself innocent—prevails. Something similar seems to have happened in the press's relationship to the Catholic Church: the assumption of good faith is no longer granted. Indeed, in some instances the new assumption is that the Catholic Church is, by its nature and structure, duplicitous. (That false assumption explains why, when a 1962 Roman instruction on dealing confidentially with priests who solicited sexual favors in the confessional was brought to public attention in 2003, reporters could present it as "smoking gun" explaining the "cover-ups" of clerical sexual abuse in recent years, contrary to the text of the document itself or any reasonable interpretation of it.) More often than not, the Church's dealings with the press are clumsy and defensive, which means that the new suspiciousness on the part of reporters and editors is not entirely the press's fault. But insofar as an assumption of mendacity is now the press's default position in matters Catholic, it is something that only the press can correct. Moreover, if that attitude of permanent suspicion turns out to be rooted in an even deeper suspicion about life-forming and culture-challenging religious conviction, then that, too, is a prejudice that must be named for what it is and rooted out.

Finally, there is the culture of dissent within the Church.

For two years now, the proponents of Catholic Lite have flatly denied any linkage between their works and the crisis of 2002, dismissing that analysis as overwrought or politically contrived. Yet not a single critic of this analysis, from within the culture of dissent, has assayed a comprehensive alternative explanation of the causalities involved in the Long Lent of 2002. There has been much evocation of the "complexity" of it all; but there has been no serious wrestling with the complex argument, or the complex set of recommendations for authentic Catholic reform, offered here and elsewhere. Instead, the same tired mantras are repeated, to the effect that only when Catholicism becomes more like a liberal Protestant denomination will these problems be resolved. That "these problems" are thoroughly unresolved in liberal Protestant denominations goes unremarked, not surprisingly. All of which suggests that the Lite Brigade continues its headlong charge into the valley of irrelevance.

As for the growing wheat in the Catholic Church in the United States, perhaps the best way to describe it is through a personal story. Six months into the Long Lent of 2002, during the editing of this book, my wife and I hosted an evening for about two dozen young priests we had gotten to know when they were students in Rome in the mid- and late-1990s. Any concerns I had about these men being depressed or knocked off balance spiritually by the bludgeoning the Church had taken in the two or three years since their ordinations were quickly dispelled. No one was sullen; no one was downhearted; no one complained. My young friends were even more committed to living out the fullness of their priesthood than they had been before. The entire evening's conversation was about the future—what was to be done, how could the process of authentic Catholic reform be accelerated? It was the happiest evening I had had in a half-year. And as I've stayed in touch with these young priests since, their commitment has remained firm. These men are neither naifs nor optimists; they're too bright to be naive, and they're too experienced to be optimists. But they remain men of hope. And they will lead the authentic reform of priestly life and formation in the United States in the decades ahead.

The wheat in the field of U.S. Catholic life is also evident in the many thousands of new Catholics who have come into the Church in the past two years. When conversions increase during a period in which the institutional Church is being publicly pilloried, one gets a sense of the enduring vitality of a Catholicism in which the treasure of compelling and life-transforming truth is always held in earthen vessels. There has been a deterioration of Catholic practice in some dioceses in the United States; but they seem to be a distinct minority. Then, in addition to new Catholics and faithful older Catholics, there are the kids. In the fifteen months since this book was first published I have spoken on several dozen campuses, including bastions of the Catholic culture of dissent. In every case, without exception, it is the students who are most receptive to the challenge of authentic Catholic reform. The same is true on secular campuses, where Catholic undergraduates who want to live a fully and authentically Catholic life are openly defying the regnant culture of debonair nihilism. They may get odd looks; they may even be persecuted by more aggressive faculty members. But they are there, their numbers are increasing, and they're not backing off the arguments.

That receptivity to a challenge to authentic Catholic reform is mirrored in the various Catholic renewal groups and associations I've addressed in the past two years. As I proposed above, many, many Catholics want to be summoned to lives of heroic virtue. They are waiting for bishops and priests to call them to the spiritual and moral greatness that, by God's grace, is their baptismal destiny. But with or without an official summons, Catholics whose stories never make the newspapers or the TV news have decided that the best way they can deal with the Long Lent of recent years is to lead the most fully Catholic lives possible. As their numbers multiply, so will the opportunities for turning crisis-as-cataclysm into crisis-as-opportunity.

That the wheat must always live beside the weeds until the final ingathering is not, of course, a reason for complacency. Effective Catholic leadership can mitigate the poisonous effects of the weeds on the wheat; effective Catholic leadership can even lessen the likelihood of the weeds propagating themselves. That leadership will only be forthcoming, however, when the pastoral authorities of the Church understand that no corners toward authentic Catholic reform have been turned because a canonical framework has been established for handling charges of sexual misconduct by priests, or because the "Catholic crisis" is no longer a front-page story every day in the newspapers. To vary Churchill, getting a long-overdue canonical framework in place and keeping the national media at bay are not even the end of the beginning; and they are certainly not the beginning of the end. The end of the beginning of the path to authentic Catholic reform is a recognition that the breakdown of priestly discipline and episcopal governance that created the Catholic crisis of 2002 began with a breakdown in fidelity. And, to say it once again, the only answer to a crisis of fidelity is fidelity—unapologetic, unambiguous, enthusiastic fidelity to the fullness of Catholic truth.

G.W.
December 12, 2003
Feast of Our Lady of Guadalupe,
Patroness of the Americas

ACKNOWLEDGMENTS

Many friends and colleagues have had a part in the preparation of this book by sharing insights, memoranda, materials, conversation, and, most importantly, solidarity amid the Catholic crisis of 2002. I am happy to acknowledge their contributions here: John Allen; Cardinal William W. Baum; Jody Bottum; Richard Boudreaux; Don Briel; Monsignor Charles Brown; Father Romanus Cessario, O.P.; Monsignor James Conley; Father Raymond De Souza; Father Joseph Augustine DiNoia, O.P.; Cardinal Avery Dulles, S.J.; Mary Eberstadt; Father Brian Farrell, L.C.; Monsignor Thomas Fucinaro; Mary Ann Glendon; Carter Griffin; Germain Grisez; Bishop James M. Harvey; Melinda Henneberger; Father Mark Knestout; Gary Kozel; Father Matthew Lamb; Father Roger Landry; Elizabeth Lev; Bishop William E. Lori; Francis X. Maier; Father Paul Mankowski, S.J.; Father Robert McClory; Father Timothy McMorland; Father Timothy Moyle; Father Christopher Nalty; Father Richard John Neuhaus; Father Jay Scott Newman; Ambassador James Nicholson; Suzanne Nicholson; Michael Novak; Archbishop George Pell; Robert Royal; Father Michael Sherwin, O.P.; Father K. Bartholomew Smith; Cardinal J. Francis Stafford; Monsignor Daniel Thomas; Bishop Allen H. Vigneron; and Father Thomas Williams, L.C.

Some of the ideas here were first tested in my weekly column, "The Catholic Difference"; I thank all those at the *Denver Catholic Register* who are responsible for the column's syndication, especially Greg Kail.

Ever Johnson, my assistant, read the manuscript with care and insight. She and Dee Roed kept my office under control while I was working on this project. I should also like to thank my friend and colleague, Dr. Hillel Fradkin, president of the Ethics and Public Policy Center, for seeing this book as a crucial part of the Center's work.

As always, my thanks to the priests and people of St. Jane Frances de Chantal Parish in Bethesda, Maryland, for their friendship and their support in prayer.

Elizabeth Maguire, my editor, and her colleagues at Basic Books have been stalwart supporters of this book from the beginning. Lori Hobkirk did a fine job of copyediting. I am also grateful, as always, for the skill and counsel of my agent, Loretta Barrett.

And, of course, my love and gratitude go to my wife, Joan, and to Gwyneth, Monica, and Stephen.

G. W.
June 29, 2002
Solemnity of Saints Peter and Paul

INDEX

Pornography. *See* Catholic
Church, and pornography;
Protestant, pornography
problem
Porter, James, 82, 92
priestly education, 177–181, 183
priestly identity, 22–28, 147–148,
171, 174–177, 178, 181,
188, 196
priests. *See* Catholic Church,
2002 crisis in, discipleship;
Catholic Church, 2002
crisis in, fidelity; Catholic
Church, 2002 crisis in,
sexual abuse; Catholic
Church, and celibacy;
Catholic Church, asceticism
in; Catholic Church,
comradery, fraternity, and
clubbiness in; Catholic
Church, need for reform in
(priesthood); Catholic
Church, vocational
recruitment in; laity and
priests; priestly education;
priestly identity; women
and priesthood; other
specific topics
Protestant
bureaucratization, 98, 213
pornography problem, 21
Reformation, 3, 4, 5, 27
sexual abuse, 21, 36

psychotherapy. *See* Catholic
Church, and psychotherapy

Ratzinger, Cardinal Joseph, 88,
89, 90, 138, 139
Re, Cardinal Giovanni Battista,
138, 139
Reese, Father Thomas, S.J., 214
reform. *See* Catholic Church,
need for reform in
ressourcement movement, 220, 222
Rieff, Philip, 102
Roberts, Father Mark, 16
Robichaud, Father George, 17
Roe v. Wade, 106
Roman Curia, 27, 87, 120–123,
128, 129, 131, 134, 135,
215
Rome. *See* Catholic Church, 2002
crisis in, and Rome
(Vatican); Catholic Church,
structure of authority in;
Roman Curia; Second
Vatican Counsel
(1962–1965); Vatican; other
specific topics
Rooney, Father Donald F.,
12–13

de Sales, Saint Francis, 199, 205,
208
San Francisco Chronicle, 16
Sartre, Jean-Paul, 62